Decorative Details

Contents

Storage and Screens 56

Lampshades 66

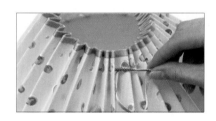

Tools and Techniques 74

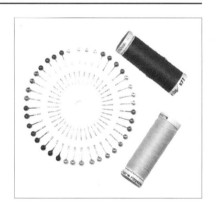

Very easy

A little skill

Some experience

Before you Begin

Creating successful soft furnishings relies in part on the right choice of fabrics and trimmings. This chapter outlines the most important factors to consider when choosing fabrics, including tips on the effective use of colour and pattern in creating a particular look or style and advice on choosing an appropriate weight and type of fabric.

Practical considerations such as how to work out the quantities of material that you need and how to match the designs of patterned fabrics perfectly across widths are fully explained.

This chapter introduces the basic ingredients of the projects - fabrics, interlinings and trimmings - giving all the information necessary to choose the right products for each item that you make.

Style and colour

A successful room scheme tells us something about the personalities of the people in whose home it appears but it also relies on using the basic principles of style and colour to show off the room to the best possible advantage.

IMPROVING ON A ROOM'S NATURAL POSITION AND SHAPE

▲ Sunny rooms may be too bright and stimulating and need a cooler look, in which case use pastel shades of calming blue or restful green.

▲ Cold rooms with little sunlight appear brighter and warmer if you introduce sunny colours like yellow, orange and red which are also stimulating.

◄ Large rooms offer the scope to use bright colours and bold patterns effectively. It is still wise to balance large designs with smaller co-ordinating patterns, checks, stripes or plain colours.

◄ High ceilings appear lower if they are decorated in dark colours. Dark flooring and furniture also bring floor and ceiling together. Horizontal stripes on window treatments and upholstered furniture lower the apparent height of the room too.

▲ Small rooms can easily appear claustrophobic but if you stick to pale tones on walls, ceiling and floor they instantly look more spacious. Use floor length curtains or blinds that match the wall colour. Soften colours where necessary by introducing a light-coloured rug or hanging.

▶ Low ceilings will appear further away if you use vertical stripes for walls and window treatments.

EFFECTIVE USE OF COLOUR

Next time it rains while the sun is shining, study the colours in a rainbow, how they follow and blend into each other. By joining the ends of the rainbow to make a circle the colour wheel is formed and this is used as the basis for colour planning.

The simplest scheme uses one colour only, in many shades. This is known as a monochromatic scheme. Colours that adjoin are known as closely related colours and work well together. Look at the colours that lie on either side of the main colour used in the room and pick these for a subtle addition. The complementary colour is the colour that lies directly opposite on the colour wheel and is its strongest possible contrast. A complementary colour should only be used in small quantities and is ideal for accessories, borders and piping or for decoration, such as bows and flowers.

Choosing fabrics

We are almost always drawn to a fabric by its colour and design but, before making final decisions, there are other points to bear in mind. What is the fabric made of? Can it be washed or must it be dry cleaned? Is it tough enough to do the job it is intended to do and how well will it last? And finally, will it look good in the location it is intended for?

KNOWING YOUR FIBRES

Knowing the fibres that are included in a fabric, and the advantages and disadvantages of each, helps you to choose the best fabric. Fabrics may be produced from natural or man-made fibres, or a mix of both.

Natural fibres include cotton, linen, silk and wool. These fibres are resistant to dust and dirt and clean well though some shrink when washed. Linen and silk can crease easily.

Man-made fibres may be totally synthetic like polyester, nylon and acrylics. They are usually easy to wash, are crease and shrink resistant and tough. However, they attract dust and dirt and need regular cleaning. Man-made fibres are often mixed with natural fibres so that the fabric contains the benefits of each. Some man-made fibres come from plant material, which is then chemically treated. Rayon falls into this category. This type of fibre has many of the advantages and disadvantages of totally synthetic fibres but is not as tough.

CHECKING FABRIC SUITABILITY

Before buying fabric ensure that it is suitable for the job you want it to do. Fabrics fall into one of three categories. Most are suitable for light wear like curtains, cushions, and tablecloths. For loose covers you need a tougher, close-woven fabric and only specially tough fabric is suitable for the hard wear that upholstery receives.

Remember that if you pick a fabric with a large design you will need to match the pattern when joining widths of fabric and possibly centre the design on items such as cushions. Always check the size of the pattern repeat before buying, as fabrics with bold motifs can sometimes involve considerable amounts of extra fabric, making them an expensive choice.

When making table linen or anything else that needs frequent washing, make sure that the fabric is simple to launder.

Crease up a corner of fabric in your hand, then release it to check whether the creases fall out or the fabric remains crumpled.

Thick fabrics are difficult to sew. If you are making something which includes piping in the seams, avoid them.

BUYING CHECKLIST

It is a good idea to carry out some simple checks in the shop before you buy fabric. Most fabrics carry labels with information on fibres, recommended uses, plus cleaning instructions. If any information you need is not listed ask the stockist.

- Check colour compatibility against carpet, paint and fabric samples from the room.
- If a fabric has not been pre-shrunk and is likely to shrink, buy a 30cm (12in) length to do a shrink test.
- Look for flame-resistant fabrics for covering upholstered furniture or for children's rooms.
- Stain-resistant finishes are useful on furnishings that are not convenient to wash regularly.
- Check the length of fabric carefully for flaws.
- Make sure that the pattern has been printed on to the fabric straight and follows the fabric grain.

HOME CHECKS

Having found a suitable fabric, it is well worth buying a sample and taking it home to look at the effect in the room where you want to use it. This might avoid making an expensive mistake in the long run. Look at the fabric in both day and night light as colours can appear quite different in artificial light.

PREPARING FABRIC

Before cutting out fabric press it and ensure that the top edge, cut in the shop, is straight with the grain of the fabric. Lay the fabric out on a flat area and place a set square or other square-cornered object, like a book, on the top edge to get a right angle. Extend the top edge of the right angle with a metre (yard) rule and draw a line along the fabric with tailor's chalk. Cut along the top edge following the drawn line and remove selvedges down either side.

Using patterned fabrics

Introducing pattern in soft furnishings adds character and sparkle to a room scheme. Choosing the main fabric first can provide a basis for an easy to put together room scheme. Mixing patterns is easy with so many co-ordinating fabrics available but it needs careful planning to decide how and where to use each design. Once the fabrics are chosen you need to work out the best arrangement of the design and the quantities of fabric required. A patterned fabric, matched accurately across the widths, hides seamlines in a way that is impossible on a plain one.

PLANNING A ROOM SCHEME

◄ If you are starting from scratch one of the easiest and most effective ways of planning a scheme is to choose a fabric and use this as the basis for the scheme.

◄ The way that a room is used affects the choice of patterns. Bold designs and bright colours are welcoming and are ideal for bathrooms, and for open areas like a hall or stairs. For rooms where you spend more time, such as bedrooms or living rooms choose a more relaxing background.

▲ The fabric design you choose can change the apparent shape of a room. Bold designs such as this one make an area appear smaller, while small designs can increase the spacious look.

◄ Use co-ordinating patterns to create an integrated scheme. For an individual effect, pick a colour, then mix florals, stripes or checks, all based on it.

◄ Choose vertical stripes, as here, if you want to add height, or horizontal stripes if you want to add width or length.

PATTERN REPEAT

◄ When buying fabric with bold designs you need to work out how much extra fabric you will need to position the design in the best way possible and to match it across fabric widths. Check the length of the pattern repeat. On curtains the lower edge of the design should be on the hem edge, on a tablecloth, wall hanging or mat the design is best centred. On a chair the design needs to be centred to outer chair back, inner chair back, seat cushions and front edge plus matched on inside and outside arms.

BUYING AND USING PATTERNED FABRIC

To estimate fabric quantities accurately, cut out paper pattern pieces for all the sections. Then mark out an area on the table or floor that is the fabric's width and sub divide this into pattern repeat lengths. Arrange the pattern pieces within this area, checking that these are centred on the design or are mirror images where necessary. When satisfied with the arrangement, measure the length covered by the pattern pieces to get the quantity of fabric required. Remember to allow for the fact that the starting point on the shop's fabric length could be at any point in the design.

When joining lengths of patterned fabric the design needs to follow through on all the widths. The best way to ensure that the match is accurate is to join widths using ladder stitch (see page 78). This stitch, done from the right side, ensures that the match is accurate and when the fabric is turned to the wrong side a line of tacking is seen, ready for seams to be machine stitched.

Interfacings and linings

Some soft furnishings need stiffness and support, others need extra thickness, insulation, added softness or weight. There is a range of specially produced materials to create whichever result you require. Most come in both dark and pale shades. Choose pale alternatives under light colour fabrics and deeper shades under dark fabrics.

INTERFACINGS AND INTERLININGS

Interfacings

These are attached to the wrong side of the main fabric to provide stiffness, shape and support and are usually hidden by a lining. Match interfacing to main fabric in weight and laundering instructions.

Both sew-in or iron-on varieties of interfacing are available in a wide range of weights. Sew-in interfacings are more time consuming to apply but, because they allow some movement, create a more natural result. They can be used to add body to fabrics, like plastic laminate and metallic cloth, which could be ruined by the use of a hot iron.

Interfacings may be woven or non-woven. The non-woven material is usually firmer than the woven alternative and does not fray. Woven interfacings, which contain some stretch, are ideal for use with fabrics that are cut on the bias.

Interlinings

Placed between the main fabric and lining, interlinings add insulation, thickness and weight. Available in wide widths, they are ideal for use with larger items such as curtains. Bump, a woven interlining made from cotton or a mix of cotton and viscose, is best used for light curtains or for quilting. Cotton domette, which is smoother and finer, is also used for quilting or for interlining medium-weight curtains. A thicker ribbed interlining which is a cotton/viscose/polymide mixture, and a cheaper alternative known as raised interlining made from viscose and nylon, are also available.

APPLYING INTERFACINGS

Sew-in interfacings

Light to medium-weight interfacings can be included in the seam. Simply tack the interfacing to the wrong side of the fabric, and make up as usual. Firm and heavyweight interfacings are sewn inside the seamlines. To do this, cut out the interfacing to match the fabric, then trim off the seam allowance. Place on the wrong side of the fabric, with outer edges just inside the seamlines. Tack in place, then herringbone stitch the interlining in position. Make up as usual.

Iron-on interfacings

Very lightweight iron-on interfacings can be caught in with the seam but interfacings of a heavier weight should be cut to fit just inside the seamlines.

To fix, place the interfacing with the adhesive side down on the wrong side of the fabric. Cover with a damp cloth and, using a dry iron on a warm setting, press for about 15 seconds on one area at a time. Do not slide the iron across the fabric. Leave to cool. On heavier fabrics, turn the fabric over and press again on the right side.

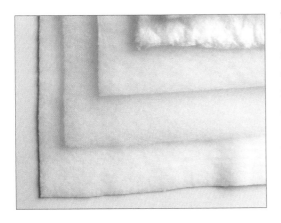

WADDINGS

Waddings, which add bulk and insulation, come in both natural and man-made fibres. Cotton wadding has a layer of fluffy material sandwiched between thin layers of cotton fabric. Use it with silk and other fine fabrics when hand quilting. Cotton wadding must be dry cleaned.

Polyester wadding is washable. It comes in a number of weights. The most commonly used are: lightweight 50g (2oz) for use in appliqué, medium-weight 100g (4oz) for quilting and heavyweight 200g (8oz) used for bed quilts. Polyester wadding can also be used to stuff small items.

LININGS

A lining not only neatens the wrong side but also provides form and body and protects the main fabric from light and dirt. Choose the best lining that you can afford as a poor quality lining will wear out long before the main fabric. Cotton sateen is the most widely used lining fabric. It comes in two widths, 120cm (48in) and 137cm (54in), and in a wide range of colours as well as white and neutrals. Both easy-care polyester/cotton and wide-width cotton poplin can also be used as linings.

Trimmings and Tiebacks

Handmade trimmings like piping, frills, plaits and bows are not difficult to produce, yet add the finishing touch that turns a plain home furnishing into an exciting design that is unique to you. The effect a trimming creates depends on its colour and shape and where you place it. It can be used to match a furnishing scheme, co-ordinate with it or add a dramatic contrast.

These trimmings are easy to add to ready-made soft furnishings and simple shapes are quickly enhanced with frills, bows or a bold plaited edge.

All of the trimmings featured in this chapter have an extra bonus. They can be quickly added to, or used to create, curtain tiebacks, making a practical and attractive decoration for your home.

Trimming styles

Tiebacks decoratively hold curtains away from the window. To create the effect you want, decisions need to be made about the position of the tiebacks in relation to the shape of the window, the drape of the fabric and the length of the curtain.

Consider whether you want to use tiebacks to highlight the curtain treatment, to show off a pretty window, reveal a beautiful view or to let in or exclude light. All these factors affect the position of the tiebacks. Before making a decision, test the alternative effects with a strip of fabric or string held at various levels around the curtains.

Each of the trimmings in this chapter can be used to embellish and add individuality to home furnishings.

TIEBACK CHOICES

For a neat and subtle border to seams or edges, traditional smooth piping is very effective or, for a more unusual finish, ruched piping is simple as well as decorative.

A generous single bow can highlight a decorative effect like a pleat or flounce. A line of small bows can accentuate a shaped edge.

TIEBACK POSITIONS

A tieback is traditionally positioned about two-thirds down a curtain's length. This is ideal if you want to show off curtain fabric or rich draping, as curtains can remain pulled across the window at the top and simply held back lower down with tiebacks.

Use a single curtain, rather than a pair, tied back to one side of the window to create stunning impact.

However, on decorative windows: those with a beautiful view or in a dark room, this is unlikely to be a viable option.

ATTACHING TIEBACKS

The simplest way to fix a tieback to a wall or window frame is to use a screw hook, and many attractive designs are available. To fix into wood, it is only necessary to start the hole with a bradawl and a hammer before screwing in the hook. When screwing into a wall, it is important to use a plastic wall plug. First drill a hole, tap in the wall plug until the end is flush with the wall and then screw the hook into the centre.

On a small or short window try placing tiebacks one-third of the way down full-length curtains, or two-thirds the way down sill-length curtains. This allows the maximum amount of light into the room, as does hanging curtains as far back to each side of the window as possible.

The third choice for a full length curtain is to place the tiebacks half-way down the curtain or at sill level, if the window is short. This shows off balanced swirls of fabric above and below the tieback.

CHECKING THE SIZE

Once you have decided on the tieback position, lightly mark the spot for the fixing on the wall, and hold a tape measure around the curtain at this point. Ensure that the measure allows the amount of drape you want, adjust if necessary, then note the length on the tape. This measurement is the length of your finished tieback.

Smooth piping

Piping is the traditional method of creating a neat, classic finish to an edge or seam on many soft furnishings. Use it to outline cushions and tiebacks, highlight chair and sofa seams, edge pelmets, curtains and blinds or to act as a colour divide between furnishing fabrics, frills and pleats.

To form a smooth, rounded edge, piping cord is sandwiched within the piping fabric. Where a flat finish is required, fabric alone can be used without the addition of piping cord.

MATERIALS:
Furnishing fabrics, piping cord, matching thread, tailor's chalk
Plus for tiebacks: Heavyweight interfacing

FABRIC:
For piping: Measure all the seamlines and edges to be piped and add these measurements together. Include an additional 5cm (2in) for each join to give the total length of fabric strips and piping cord required. Allow for shrinkage when using cotton piping cord and wash before using. Fabric used for piping is cut on the bias in strips 5cm (2in) wide (see below).
For tiebacks: Make up the pattern to your required size (see pages 90-91). You will need two pieces of fabric this size, or one of fabric and one of lining, and one piece of interfacing plus two 46cm (18in) lengths of 2.5cm (1in) wide ribbon for ties. Alternatively, make up ties from lengths of piping fabric cut 8cm (3in) wide.

MAKING PIPING

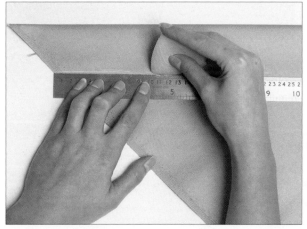

1 To cut out bias strips, first fold the fabric at a 45 degree angle. To do this, lay the fabric flat with selvedges to right and left. Take one of the top corners and fold it across to the opposite selvedge. Press to iron in the fold, then draw in parallel lines on the fabric at 5cm (2in) intervals with a piece of tailor's chalk. Cut out the strips.

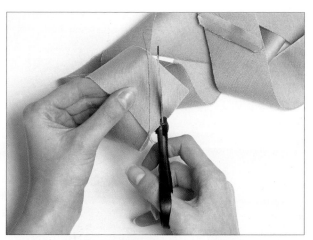

2 Join pieces of fabric to make up the length of piping required. Pin pieces together with right sides facing, then machine stitch together with narrow seams along the straight grain of the fabric. Trim the seams and then press them open. Fold the fabric strip in half lengthways with right side outside, matching raw edges.

 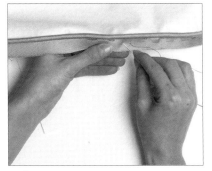 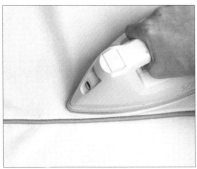

3 Encase the piping cord inside the folded strip. Pin to hold, then using a zipper foot stitch along the strip close to the cord. Leave a 1.25cm (½in) gap before stitching to allow for joining piping together.

4 Place the covered piping strip along right side of the seamline of one piece of fabric to be piped, aligning the stitchline over the seamline and matching the raw edges of fabric and piping. Pin and stitch in place.

5 With right sides together, position the second piece of fabric over the piped stitchline, with raw edges matching, and tack in place along the seamline. Stitch all sections, then turn right side out and press.

JOINING PIPING ENDS TOGETHER

Stop stitching 5cm (2in) before the ends of the piping meet up. Trim the cord to meet exactly but allow an overlap of 1.25cm (½in) of fabric beyond join. Turn fabric under 6mm (¼in) and enclose the raw fabric end at start of piping. Continue stitching across the join.

PIPED TIEBACK

1 Using pattern A on page 91, cut out a piece of interfacing to the size of the finished tieback and two pieces of fabric to tieback size plus 1.25cm (½in) seam allowance all round. Place interfacing shape centrally on the wrong side of front tieback shape and use a neat herringbone stitch (see page 79) to attach the interfacing to the fabric.

2 Make up piping to go around tieback following steps 1-3, Making Piping and stitch to right side of interfaced tieback shape following step 4. Fold in seam allowance on the second fabric piece, snipping into the allowance so that it lies flat, press, then tack. Attach one end of each strip of ribbon behind the tieback front. Slipstitch lining to back of piped tieback shape, covering all raw edges.

Ruched piping

Ruched piping is made in a similar way to smooth piping but the strip is gathered up to create the ruched finish. Use thick piping cord to create the most dramatic effect.

Fine to medium-weight fabrics that gather well are most suitable for ruched piping. Piping fabric also needs to be of a similar weight to the main fabric. Mix plain piping with patterned fabric and vice versa to create the strongest impact.

MATERIALS:
Fine to medium-weight fabric, piping cord, matching thread
Plus for tiebacks: Soft rope or extra thick cord, 2 curtain rings

FABRIC:
For piping: To calculate the length of fabric required, measure all the seamlines and edges to be piped and add these measurements together then double the final figure. Include an additional 5cm (2in) for each join. For the piping cord, use the single measurement around seams and edges. Allow for shrinkage when using cotton piping cord and wash before using. Fabric which is to be used for ruched piping is cut on the bias in strips 6.5cm (2½in) wide (see page 18).
For tiebacks: To calculate fabric required, measure the finished length for each tieback (see pages 16-17), double this length then add 2.5cm (1in) for turn-in at ends. For the width, measure around the rope or cord used and add 5cm (2in) to this measurement. For each tieback you will also need four circles of fabric twice the diameter of the cord end.

MAKING RUCHED PIPING

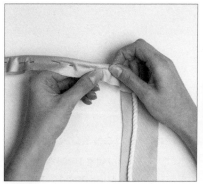

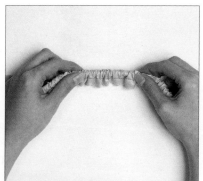

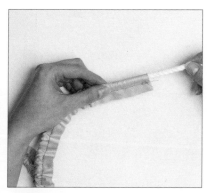

1 Make up the length of fabric required from bias strips (see steps 1 and 2, page 18). With the right side out, fold the fabric in half lengthways, matching raw edges. Place the end of the piping cord at one end of the fabric strip, encase it in the fabric, then pin along the edge to secure.

2 Using large machine stitches, stitch across the end of cord and fabric to hold them in place. Then, allowing a small space between cord and stitchline, stitch for about 20cm (8in). Stop and gently pull the cord through to create gathers in the fabric. Adjust to ensure gathers are even.

3 Hold the cord taut and continue stitching and gathering until the cord end is reached. Add extra strips if necessary. Check that the gathering is as full as you want it, then stitch across cord end with large machine stitches to hold it in place temporarily.

RUCHED TIEBACK

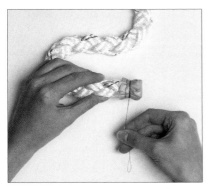

1 Cut out one fabric strip for each tieback to the required length (see Fabric). Fold the strip in half lengthways, wrong side out, and stitch along

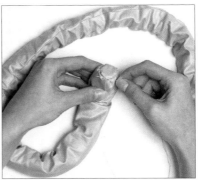

2 Pull the rope through the fabric tube to the opposite end and attach fabric circles to it, securing tube end to the fabric, as step 1.

seamline, making a fabric tube. Turn right side out and press, with seam to centre back. Tack two of the fabric circles together around the edge and place over the rope end. Stitch the circles around the sides of the rope to secure (you cannot attach to the sealed rope ends), then wind thread around the fabric-encased rope end. Stitch two lines of gathers around the tube end, pull up, turn in raw edge and slipstitch to fabric-covered end.

Adjust fabric gathers so that they are even along the length of the tieback. Attach a ring to the tieback at each end, overstitching the ring to the fabric-covered rope end to hold it in place.

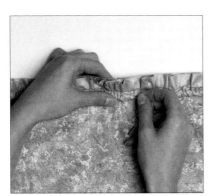

4 Adjust gathering if necessary so that it is even along the length and then attach piping to one main fabric piece (see step 4, pages 18-19). Once attached, unpick threads across the piping cord and join ends of piping together (see Joining Piping Ends Together, page 19).

PREPARING NYLON ROPE
Thick, soft nylon rope unravels quite easily. Ask the shop to cut the lengths and seal the ends for you. If you need to do this yourself, wind thread around the rope either side of the cutting point. Then, using small sharp scissors, cut through the rope one cord at a time. Seal the end immediately with a lighted spill which will melt the end together. This is best done outside.

Frills

Frills provide a final ornamental flourish to most home furnishings. They can be used to dress up curtains, add depth to a curtain valance, give a finishing flounce to a floor-length tablecloth and enhance cushion seams and tiebacks.

Match up fabrics on a frill to the rest of the furnishing that you are making, include piping in the joining seam for extra colour or use a contrasting colour for the frill.

Frill depth depends on the furnishing it is to be attached to, with larger items requiring deeper frills. Try out different frill sizes on a spare piece of fabric to see which looks best.

MATERIALS:
Fine to medium-weight furnishing fabric, matching thread
Plus for tiebacks: Heavyweight iron-on interfacing

FABRIC:
Frill depth: Between 6.5cm and 10cm (2½ and 4in). Add seam and hem allowances. Measure all edges to which the frill is to be added and double this for frill length.
For tiebacks: Make up the pattern (see pages 90-91) to your required size. You will need two pieces of fabric this size, or one of fabric and one of lining, and one piece of interfacing.

MAKING A SINGLE FRILL

1 Remove the selvedges from the frill fabric, then on the wrong side mark lines across the width with tailor's chalk to the chosen frill depth. Do this until you have enough strips to make up the full frill length, then cut them out.

2 Join the strips together using narrow French seams (see page 81) to make up the length required. Tack under a narrow double 1.25cm (½in) hem at each short end or, if the frill is continuous, use a French seam to join one end to the other.

3 Turn in a narrow double 1.25cm (½in) hem on one long edge. Stitch down short and long edge. Alternatively, use a machine satin stitch (see page 80) to cover the raw edge or bind with bias binding.

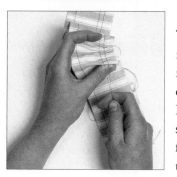

4 Using the longest stitch on the machine, run two rows of stitching along the raw edge. Stitch in lengths of about 60cm (24in). Backstitch at one end to secure and leave long threads for pulling up the gathers at the other. Pull up the gathers evenly to fit the required length. Wind threads around pins to hold. Tack the frill in position to the main fabric with raw edges matching. Stitch and neaten raw edges.

FRILLED TIEBACK

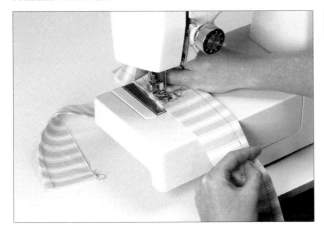 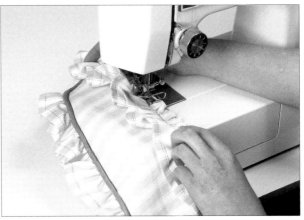

1 Cut out a curved tieback using pattern B on page 91 and make up (see step 1, Piped Tieback, pages 18-19). Cut out and make up a frill length to go around the edge of the tieback following steps 1-3, Making a Single Frill.

2 Attach piping, if required (see step 2, Piped Tieback, pages 18-19). Then, with right sides facing, match the raw edges of the tieback and frill and pin together. Tack, then stitch. Slipstitch the back of the tieback in place to cover the raw edges.

MAKING A DOUBLE FRILL

Calculate the length required in the same way as for a single frill but allow twice the depth plus a seam allowance of 2.5cm (1in). Join strips of fabric with open seams to make up the full length. Right sides together, fold the strip ends in half lengthways and stitch end seams or join to opposite end for a continuous frill. Turn right side out and refold in half along the length. Press. Stitch rows of gathering threads through both layers along the raw edge (see step 4, Making a Single Frill) and pull up the threads. Tack frill to the main fabric, stitch and then neaten raw edges.

Plaits

Plaited, padded tubes of fabric form a bold, decorative strip that can be used to stunning effect as a curtain tieback or alternatively as an edging for a floor-length tablecloth, a border for a plain bedspread or to outline the hems of curtains that sweep the floor.

Plaits are most striking if fabric of different patterns, colours or shades is used for each tube. To enhance patterned fabric, make a plait from plain fabric, picking out colours that are used in the main design.

For a co-ordinated look, use the patterned fabric for one of the strips with plain colours for the other two or use fabrics from other furnishings in the room.

MATERIALS:
Medium-weight furnishing fabric, thick wadding, matching threads
Plus for tiebacks: 2 curtain rings

FABRIC:
For a plait: Measure the finished length required. Make each fabric strip 10cm (4in) wide and the finished length plus a third to allow for take-up in the plaiting. You will need three strips of fabric cut to these measurements plus three strips of wadding 2.5cm (1in) shorter than fabric strips and only 8cm (3in) wide.
For tiebacks: Hold back the curtain and measure around it with a length of string to find the tieback length required. Follow the instructions above for plait strip sizes.

MAKING A PLAIT

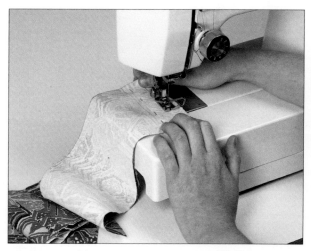

1 Cut out fabric strips. To join lengths for a longer plait place one same colour strip on top of another, with right sides together and all edges matching. Stitch across one short end 1.25cm (½in) from raw edge. Press seam open and continue in this way until you have the length required.

2 Place one strip, wrong side uppermost, with wadding positioned on top 1.25cm (½in) from short ends. Turn under one long edge of the fabric by 1.5cm (⅝in) and bring both long edges to the centre. Pin the folded edge over the long raw edge to form a tube with the wadding sandwiched inside. Slipstitch the pinned seam to hold it in place. Make up the other two tubes in the same way. Turn inside the short raw edge at one end of each tube and then slipstitch closed.

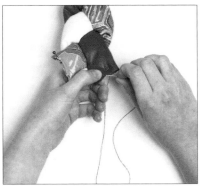

3 Overlap the three tubes at the finished end, pin and stitch them together. Temporarily hold this end firm by pinning it to an upholstered surface. Plait the three strips together, keeping the plaiting neat and fairly loose. Make sure the long slipstitched seams are at the back.

4 Continue plaiting, measuring the plait as you work, until the required length is reached. Trim off any excess if necessary, allowing for the seam allowance at raw ends. Turn the raw ends inside and pin, then slipstitch closed. Join the plait end strips together as before.

PLAITED BORDERS

If the plait is to be used as a decorative edging, along a curtain hem for example, simply slipstitch in position along the finished hem edge.

Where plaits join up, around a tablecloth or a bedspread for instance, only tack the plait ends (see steps 3 and 4). When the plait is attached to the furnishing, remove end tacking and, one at a time, slipstitch one tube end to the opposite end of the same tube to form one continuous plait.

PLAITED TIEBACK

1 Follow the instructions under Fabric for cutting the strips. Make up one plait to the required length for each curtain, see steps 1-4 above.

2 Attach a curtain ring securely to the back edge of each tieback end and hang from fixed hooks at the required height.

Bows

The addition of bows can considerably enhance plain soft furnishings. The simplest bows are tied from lengths of ribbon, cord or a sash of fabric but for a larger bow, a stronger shape is created when the bow is made in three separate sections of loops, tails and a wrapped around knot.

MATERIALS:
Furnishing fabric, matching thread
Plus for tiebacks: Iron-on interfacing, 2 large curtain rings

FABRIC:
Make a bow from scrap fabric and use this to work out your measurements.
Loops: Measure from one loop tip to the other and the loop depth. Use a piece of fabric twice the length by twice the depth, plus seam allowances.
Tails: Measure from the tip of one tail, through the knot, to the tip of the other. You need two pieces this length by the required width, plus seam allowances.
Knot: Cut a rectangular piece of fabric the circumference of the knot by twice the width of the knot, plus seam allowances.
For tiebacks: Measure around the held back curtain to calculate the length required. Cut a rectangle of fabric twice the chosen width by the length, plus seam allowances. Cut a piece of iron-on interfacing to finished tieback size.

MAKING A BOW

1 Placing right sides together, fold the loop rectangle in half lengthways. Pin and then stitch the long raw edges together. Press seam open, turn right side out and press again with the seam at the centre. Zigzag stitch across each end to secure.

2 Fold each end of the strip in to the centre, overlapping by 2.5cm (1in). Then slipstitch together to secure. Pleat up bow centre by hand and wrap thread around the centre to hold it in place.

3 For tails, place one tail piece over the other, with right sides together and pin to hold. To angle the ends, fold over one short edge so that it meets the side edge. Press to mark angle, unfold fabric and cut 1.25cm (½in) outside this line. Cut so that the angles at each end are parallel to each other. Stitch around the raw edges, leaving a 5cm (2in) gap at the centre of one long edge. Trim the seam allowance at the points, then turn right side out and press. Slipstitch the opening closed. Mark the centre of the tail piece, then stitch two rows of gathering thread at a slight angle from one edge to the other.

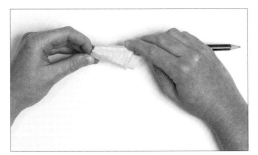

4 To make the knot piece, fold the rectangle of fabric in half along the length with right sides together. Stitch the long, raw edges to form a tube, then press. Turn the tube right side out, using a pencil to ease the fabric through. Finish ends as with the loops.

5 To assemble the bow, pull up the gathers in the tail piece to match the knot width and secure the threads. Fold the tail piece along the angled gather line, then position over the back of the loops and stitch through all thicknesses to hold. Wind the knot piece around the loops and tails to cover the gathers, overlapping the ends at the back. Trim if necessary, then fold over the seam allowance on the top edge and slipstitch in place.

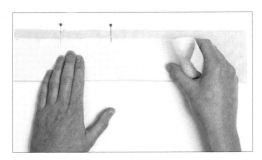

BOW-DECORATED TIEBACK

1 Fold tieback fabric, wrong side outside and position interfacing over this flush with folded edge but with fabric seam allowance showing equally on the other three sides. Iron interfacing in place following instructions (see page 13). Stitch tieback along raw edge of the long side. Turn right side out and press. Fold in raw edges at each end, insert a curtain ring in the seam and slipstitch openings closed.

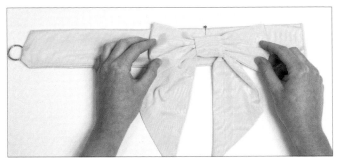

2 Make up the bow, as steps 1-4 above. The bow is positioned slightly off centre so that it appears to the front of the tieback. First find the centre of the tieback length, then mark a position about 8cm (3in) to one side of the centre. Stitch two lines of gathering threads across the tieback at this point, leaving a space of 1.25cm (½in) at top and bottom. On a pair of curtains, mark the position for the second bow to the opposite side of the centre point. Pull up and fix gathering threads to depth of bow knot and stitch back of knot to tieback with double thread.

Tassels

Tassels are fun to make, require a minimum of sewing and provide a sumptuous finish to cushions, window treatments, bedcovers and hangings as well as creating decorative tiebacks.

Knitting cotton or wool, embroidery thread and string are all suitable for making tassels.

MATERIALS:
2 balls double knitting cotton, 4cm (1⅝in) paper craft ball, tapestry needle, 15cm x 17cm (6in x 6½in) thick card rectangle, *Plus for tieback:* 1.5cm (⅝in) diameter tube (plastic or cardboard), small button with two holes

MAKING A TASSEL

1 First make a larger hole through the centre of the paper ball. Start this off with the end of small pointed scissors, then pull the paper out of the centre until the hole is 1.5cm (⅝in) all the way through.

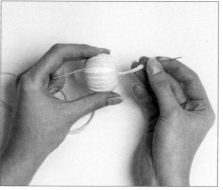

2 Thread the needle with as long a length of knitting cotton as you can manage and take this through the centre of the hole, leaving an end hanging. Continue threading the single strand of yarn through the hole and around the outside of the ball. Place the strands of yarn in pairs, leaving a small space between each pair, until the ball is covered with 25 pairs of equally spaced strands, then secure the yarn through the centre and cut off the thread.

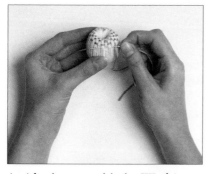

3 Thread the needle with a length of the second colour yarn, securing the knotted end neatly inside the central hole. Working around the ball, weave the yarn alternately over and under each pair of vertical strands. Continue weaving the second colour until the ball is covered with alternating strands of yarn.

4 Working with both colours at once, wind yarn around the card length about 40 times. Then thread a 30cm (12in) length of yarn under all the loops at one edge. Slip the loops off the card and tie the yarn tightly. Pass each end through one hole in the button and knot to secure. Cut the loops at the other end, then trim to form an even edge.

5 To make the fixing loop, cut three strands of cotton 104cm (41in) long. Hold together and fold the lengths in half.

Place one finger through the halfway loop and twist the lengths at the opposite end until they are tightly twisted around each other. Bring the loose ends through the loop and hold, letting the cotton twist on itself to form a cord. Stitch loose ends together to secure, leaving a length of cotton yarn.

6 Attach the sections by stitching the two ends of the twisted cord together to form a loop, then thread the cotton yarn through the centre of the ball and through the centre of the tassel tail into the holes in the button. Bring the thread back through again, finally knotting it to the end of the loop. Wind a threaded length of cotton around tassel tail and under ball to neaten and secure with a small knot or stitch.

TASSEL TIEBACK

1 Make the tassel following steps 1-5, Making a Tassel, but do not attach sections together.

2 For a 72.5cm (28½in) double-looped tieback, cut six lengths of knitting cotton 7.2m (8yd) long (to avoid raw ends, allow extra yarn and fold back at each end). Fold the six lengths in half and secure the loop around a door knob then twist together. When the strands start to wind round themselves, bring the loose ends up through the loop to make a twisted cord. Secure with thread, then form the cord into a loop. Stitch, then wind cotton over the join to neaten.

3 Cut a 2.5cm (1in) length of tube and smooth the ends if necessary. Cover the tube with cotton strands (see steps 2 and 3, Making a Tassel). To assemble the tieback, fold the cord so that the joined end is in the centre. Then push the cord through the covered tube until tube lies in the middle of the cord, covering the join. Using the needle, also thread the narrow cord which attaches to the tassel through the tube. Finally, assemble the sections of the tassel (see step 6, Making a Tassel).

Tablemats and Covers

The addition of a new tablecloth or cover can dramatically transform a worn or unattractive table. A basic cloth for everyday use is very quick to make and can be easily enhanced with the addition of decorative trimmings or shaped edges.

Tablemats are a good alternative to a cloth, particularly if you want to show off a smart table. They can be made from fabrics that complement your furnishings. Mats made from plastic laminated cloth, which can be wiped clean, are both fun and immensely practical for small children.

A floor-length tablecover, on either a rectangular or round table, can look stunning, and is a good way of transforming an inexpensive piece of furniture into something special.

Style choices and measuring

Tablecloths need not be consigned merely for practical, protective use over dining or kitchen tables. Other tables in halls, living rooms and bedrooms can be considerably enhanced by a cloth or floor-length cover. These can be as simple or as decorative as you desire. Choose the most appropriate skirt length, then add decoration with a frill (see pages 22-23) or add a plaited edge to a full length cloth (see pages 24-25) to highlight and stiffen the hem.

ALTERNATIVE SKIRT LENGTHS

▲ A short cloth is best for everyday mealtimes.

◀ For stronger impact make a cloth that drops to a length halfway between the table surface and the floor.

▲ A full length cloth is often the most decorative choice for a display table. This can either reach to floor level or you can make it slightly longer so that it drapes over the floor covering.

MEASURING A TABLE

To measure the best length for a short cloth that is used for mealtimes sit at the table. Measure the drop from table edge to just above your lap.

Square table

Measure the top from the edge on one side to the opposite edge. Add to this measurement the length of the required overhang and double it. This is the size of your finished cloth. Add seam allowances and hems.

Rectangular table

Measure the length of the table top from edge to opposite edge. Measure the width of the table top from edge to opposite edge. Add to each measurement the length of the required overhang and double it. This is the size of your finished cloth. Add seam allowance and hems.

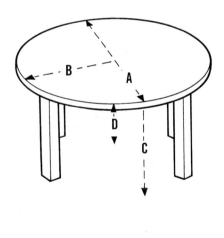

A: Table top length   **C:** Table drop
B: Table top width   **D:** Overhang

Oval table

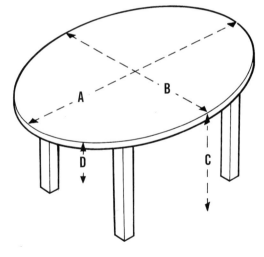

A: Table top length   **C:** Table drop
B: Table top width   **D:** Overhang

Measure the length of the table from edge to edge at the longest point. Measure the width of the table in the same way. Add to each measurement the length of the required overhang and double it. Add seam allowances and hems. This is the size of the rectangle from which the oval cloth is cut.

Round table

A: Diameter   **C:** Table drop
B: Radius   **D:** Overhang

Measure the diameter of the table top from the edge on one side to the edge on the opposite side. Add to this measurement the length of the required overhang and double it. Add seam allowances and hems. This is the size of the square from which the circular cloth is cut.

Bordered square cloth ✂

These two projects show how borders can enliven a basic square cloth. The first uses strips of fabric to create a square 'frame', which is then stitched to the main cloth. The second shows how to make a zigzag border to hang down from a fitted cloth. When adding a border, use fabric that is of the same weight and fibres as the material for the cloth itself.

It is possible that you will have to join fabric widths to make a square of fabric the right size. If this is the case, allow for a full fabric width in the centre of the table and add narrower panels of equal width on either side. This avoids having a seam down the middle of the cloth.

Co-ordinating napkins can be quickly and easily made from either the same fabric as the cloth or from the border fabric.

MATERIALS:
Easycare furnishing fabric, matching thread, co-ordinating fabric of same weight, card for zigzag template

FABRIC:
Measure the table (see pages 32-33) and work out the cloth size. Allow 1.25cm (½in) for hems.
For a border: Allow for four lengths of your chosen width, adding 2.5cm (1in) on all sides. Add extra to the length if pattern matching is required.
For a zigzag border: Measure the table top for a cloth to fit exactly and allow for eight lengths of border fabric. Each of these should be the side length plus 2.5cm (1in) and 9cm (3½in) wider than the depth of the edge shape.

APPLIED BORDER

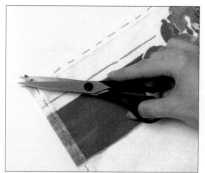

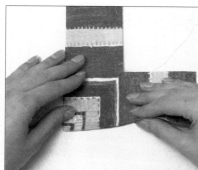

1 Cut out fabric to the required size, centring any bold design. Join widths with flat fell seams (see page 81). Turn a 1.25cm (½in) single hem on to the right side of the fabric along all sides, tack in place. Trim hem fabric on corners diagonally to lie flat.

2 Cut out four border strips. Along both long edges of each, press under a 1.25cm (½in) single hem to the wrong side. Pin lengths right sides together, tack, then machine, attaching them diagonally to form a mitre at each corner. Trim mitres.

3 To apply the border to the main fabric, place it over the right side of cloth, matching the outer edges of the cloth and the border carefully. Pin in place, tack to secure, then topstitch the border to the cloth, machining close to inner and outer edges.

ZIGZAG BORDER

1 Cut the cloth to fit the table top exactly, adding a seam allowance. Decide on the width and depth of each zigzag shape, remembering that the border should divide equally into each side of the cloth and finish with a complete shape to each side of the corner. Allow a 3.5cm (1½in) top border and 5cm (2in) for a seam allowance at border ends.

3 Cut out eight border lengths, using the pattern. With right sides together, pin, then tack pairs of border lengths together along short straight sides and zigzag edges. Stitch, clip corners, turn right side out and press. Press under 1.25cm (½in) separate hems along the top edges and tack. Repeat on all border pieces.

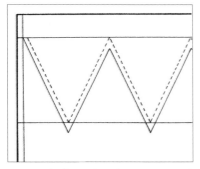

2 Make a template for the zigzag border. On a piece of card, draw a horizontal line 1.25cm (½in) from the top edge, then 3.5cm (1½in) below this draw a second horizontal line. Starting 2.5cm (1in) from the end, mark off the widths for each zigzag on this second line. Mark the depth required for the zigzags, then draw a third line across the card. Mark the point position for each shape on this line. Join up marks with a dotted stitching line and 1.25cm (½in) outside this draw in a cutting line. Cut out pattern.

4 To attach the border, first make a 1.25cm (½in) snip into cloth fabric, 1.25cm (½in) from each corner and tack under, to form a square notched out corner. Matching up border edges on each corner, encase the cloth raw edge in the tacked border edge and tack through all thicknesses. Stitch border in place.

Child's tablemat

Wipeable fabric, like PVC, is ideal to use for a child's placemat. This practical mat, shaped as a grinning black-and-white cat, should tempt any small person to enjoy mealtimes. The front paws contain two neat openings, through which the fork and spoon ends can be slotted to hold them in place, ready for use.

The details on the cat's white paws and muzzle are topstitched in black before the pieces are attached to the main shape. These shapes are positioned with glue rather than pins, which would mark the fabric, before being stitched in place.

MATERIALS:

PVC fabrics in black and white, matching threads, adhesive tape, tailor's chalk, tracing paper for pattern, dressmaker's pencil, vinyl bonding adhesive, carbon paper, adhesive tape, talcum powder or tissue paper

FABRIC:

Main shape: Black PVC or other wipeable fabric 46cm x 30cm (18in x 12in)
Features: White PVC or other wipeable fabric 10cm (4in) x fabric width for the muzzle, eyes, ear centres and front paws.
Collar and disc: 15cm (6in) length of 2cm (¾in) wide adhesive tape.

MAKING THE PATTERN

Enlarge the cat shape (see page 90) by 200% on a photocopier, until it is 43cm x 29cm (17¼in x 11½in). From this pattern trace off two copies. Shade in the areas of one colour only on each pattern; the main body, back paw, head and tail on the first, and the muzzle, front paws, ear centres and eyes on the second.

1 Cut out the main shape from black PVC. On the back of the pattern, draw over the lines for the tail and back paw with a dressmaker's pencil. Place the pattern over the PVC right side up and trace over the shapes again to transfer the lines on to the material. Machine topstitch over the lines in black, stitching twice to give them more strength if necessary.

2 Transfer the paw shapes on to the white PVC, as in step 1, and machine topstitch in black. Then cut out the paws. Mark a slot wide enough to take a piece of cutlery along the top edge of each paw, then apply vinyl bonding adhesive down the sides of the paws and stick down. When dry, stitch in matching thread, leaving the cutlery slots free.

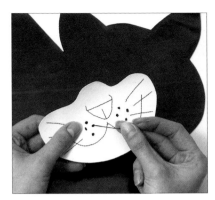

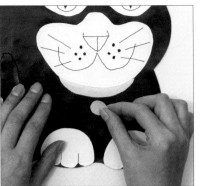

3 Cut out the muzzle and, using carbon paper behind the pattern, lightly mark in feature details on the fabric (these can be removed with damp tissue paper). Topstitch the features in black, securing threads on the wrong side. Make round whisker marks with French knots (see page 80). Then use vinyl bonding adhesive to stick the muzzle in place. When it is dry, topstitch in white thread close to the edge.

4 Cut out the ear centre triangles, glue in place on the mat, then topstitch in white. For the eyes, transfer the eye shapes on to white PVC and glue a black triangle in the centre of each eye for the pupil. Use topstitching in black to create the outline around the pupil and to stitch the pupil. Cut out the eyes and glue in position on the face. Outline eye main shape in white. Snip off any long threads with scissors.

5 For the collar and disc, cut out the shapes from adhesive tape. Remove backing paper and fix in position around the neck. This striking, wipe clean mat is now ready for use. To give a highly individual effect, initials can be embroidered on the collar disc in coloured thread.

WORKING WITH PVC

Fix shapes in position with glue or adhesive tape rather than pins, which mark the fabric.

When stitching use a ball point needle, a long stitch and a roller foot if you have one. If the fabric sticks to the foot when topstitching, dust it with talcum powder or alternatively stitch through tissue paper.

Only iron PVC fabric on the wrong side with a cool iron. Always test the iron on a scrap of fabric before starting.

Quilted placemat

Using placemats allows you to show off the surface of a smart table. Here a fabric with a distinct motif has been chosen and areas of the design have been picked out with quilting. The wadding used for the quilting also provides some protection to the table surface below.

A second fabric is used to bind the edge of the placemats. This fabric is also used for napkins which have an appliqué corner design taken from the mat fabric.

MATERIALS:
Medium-weight furnishing fabric, medium-weight wadding, matching threads, paper for pattern

FABRIC:
Placemats: For four oval mats 55cm x 36cm (22in x 14in) you will need 160cm (1¾yd) of 122cm (48in) wide fabric. Allow extra to centre a bold motif on the top side of each mat and for cut-out motifs for the napkins. You will also need four pieces of wadding the same size as the mats.
Napkins: For four napkins 46cm (18in) square you will need 1m (1¼yd) fabric, plus 3.6m (4yd) for the bias border strips for the mats.

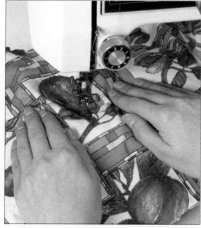

1 Cut a rectangle of paper to the size of the finished mat, allowing a little extra for take up in quilting. Fold the paper into four, then on the long folded edge mark the distance that is equal to the length of the short folded edge. Position the edge of a large plate over the open corner, between the outer corner and the mark. Draw in the curve, then cut along this line. Open up the pattern piece.

2 Using the template, cut out two oval shapes from the fabric, ensuring that the main design is centred. Allow an extra 1.25cm (½in) for seam allowances. Then use the template to cut out a piece of wadding. Position the wadding between the two fabric pieces and tack together with large stitches. Start at the centre and tack out to each curved corner.

3 Select an attractive motif from the fabric design to use as the basis of the quilting pattern. Using a large machine stitch, stitch around the outline of the shape. Alternatively, machine in diagonal lines approximately 2.5cm (1in) apart across the placemat to create a simple diamond quilting pattern.

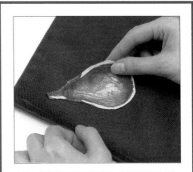

4 Measure around the edge of the template. Add 2.5cm (1in) to this measurement for joining. Then cut out bias strips for edging the mat (see pages 18-19) and join them on the straight grain to make the required length. Press each border strip in half along the length with right side out. Open out and fold the raw edge along each side in to the centre. Press in folds.

5 Open out the binding strip and place one of its raw edges to the raw edge of the mat with right sides facing. Pin the binding around the mat edge, positioning the join along the lower edge. Tack, then stitch together. Turn the binding to the other side of the mat, enclosing the raw edge. Tack, then slipstitch binding in place. To join the ends of the piping see pages 18-19.

CO-ORDINATING NAPKINS
Cut out napkins from border fabric. Then cut out and apply motifs from main fabric to one corner of each napkin fabric square, using double-sided iron-on interfacing. Satin stitch in place (see page 80). Turn under a narrow hem on all sides of the table napkin and stitch to finish.

Rectangular tablecover

This floor-length cover, which is designed to fit over a table top and sides, is an ideal way to conceal an unattractive table.

Using the diagram on page 33, measure the table and calculate fabric requirements. Use these measurements to make up a paper pattern for all the sections, clearly labelling each. Making paper pattern pieces enables you to centre any motifs and ensures that the pattern will match across each of the sections when the cover is made up.

MATERIALS:

Closely woven furnishing fabric, contrasting fabric for pleats and bows, matching sewing threads

FABRIC:

To calculate fabric requirements refer to diagram on pages 32-33
Table top: One piece A x B plus 2.5cm (1in) added to each measurement for seam allowances.
Table sides: Two pieces A x C plus 2.5cm (1in) for seam allowances and 2.5cm (1in) for hem: two pieces B x C plus 2.5cm (1in) for seam allowances and 2.5cm (1in) for hem.
Corner pleats: Four pieces C x 70cm (28in)
Bows: (see fabric details pages 26-27). Rectangles of fabric for bows shown here measure as follows: loops 60cm x 60cm (24in x 24in); tails 60cm (24in) by table drop, less 10cm (4in); knot 15cm x 11.5cm (6in x 4½in). Allow extra material to match up a design with bold motifs.

1 Using the measurements you have taken, make a paper pattern for each section. Arrange these on the straight grain of the fabric, centring motifs. Check pattern match, then cut out.

2 First make the skirt. With right sides together, pin and tack pleat pieces to each end of a side panel. Stitch together with French seams (see page 81). Repeat for the other side panel. Then join these two sections by stitching one of the end panels to the opposite edge of one corner pleat piece. Repeat with the last end piece to form a ring of joined rectangles, alternating pleat sections and side pieces.

3 With right sides together, bring the seam on one side of the pleat piece up to the seam on the opposite side. Match seams, then mark the centre of the pleat with a pin. Stitch down the seamline for 10cm (4in) to hold pleat top. Position this short pleat seam over the centre point marked by the pin. Pin together, tack to secure, then stitch along the top seamline to hold both sides of the pleat in position. Repeat for all corner pleats.

4 Neaten raw edges of table top section and top edge of skirt. Place right sides of top and skirt pieces together, matching up pleat centres to each corner of the top section. Pin, tack, then stitch with a flat seam and press seam open. Neaten corners to lie flat. Place the cover on the table and turn up a single 1.25cm (½in) hem, then a further 2.5cm (1in) hem or to the drop you require. Pin, tack, then stitch hem in place.

5 To make the bows see pages 26-27. Alternatively decorate just one or two corner pleats with an arrangement of flowers (see page 43). Position each bow or flower group over the top seam on the pleat and hand stitch in place. Press and put the cover on the table.

FLARED CORNERS

As an alternative to box pleats at the corners of the tablecover, make flared pleats.

Cut four triangular pieces 70cm (28in) wide at the lower edge tapering to a 2.5cm (1in) wide cut-off corner point at the top. Make each piece the length of the table drop plus 3.5cm (1½in) for the seam allowance. Curve the lower edge of each piece. Attach to the table side pieces in the same way as step 2. Join flare side seams for 20cm (4in) as step 3 and join top to sides as step 4. Then hem the skirt.

Lined circular cloth

A circular cloth is made from a square of fabric. For a very small table, the initial square can be made from one piece of material. For a larger cloth, it will be necessary to join widths of fabric to make a square the required size. To avoid an unsightly seam down the centre of the cloth, use the full width of fabric across the centre and part widths on either side. This ensures the seams occur near the edge of the table top or in the drop itself.

Use the diagram on page 33 to calculate the size of fabric square needed, adding extra to the length if you want the cloth to drape over the floor.

MATERIALS:
Light to medium-weight furnishing fabric, light to medium-weight lining fabric, narrow festoon blind tape, matching threads, string, drawing pin and pencil

FABRIC:
Add together the distance across the table top and twice the distance from table top to floor. Make a square of fabric this size, allowing for seam allowances on each joined piece. Make the lining the same size as the cloth. Tape length is the cloth drop measurement plus 2.5cm (1in).

1 To join fabric widths, cut one full width of top fabric to the required length. Using ladder stitch (see page 78) match the pattern and tack part widths of fabric to either side to make up a square. Stitch seams. Make up the lining in the same way.

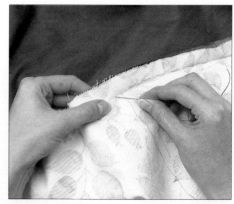

3 Place the square of lining material flat, then place the top fabric over it with right sides together. Pin to secure, then cut out the lining using the top fabric as a template. Tack, then stitch together around the edge leaving an opening of 20cm (8in) to turn the cloth through to the right side. Clip the seam at approximately 8cm (3in) intervals to ensure the edge lies flat. Turn through, press and slipstitch opening closed.

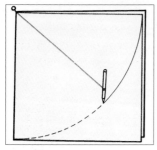

2 With right sides together, fold the top fabric in half, then half again. Cut a piece of string a little longer than the required radius of the cloth plus 1.25cm (½in) to allow for the hem seam. Make a knot at one end of the string and attach a marking pencil to the other. Check the distance between the two is the correct length, then attach the knotted end of the string to central fold corner with a pin, pull the string taut and draw in an arc from corner to corner. Cut along this line and open up the fabric.

4 To add a side flounce, as shown here, fold the cloth into four again, making sure that the lining side is outermost. To locate where the table drop begins, measure from the centre fold along one fold line a distance which is equal to the radius of the table top. Mark this point with a pin, then also mark the hem edge on the fold with a pin. The distance between the two is equal to the table drop. Open out the fabric.

5 Remove the rings that come with the tape. Fold under 1.25cm (½in) at each end of the tape, then position it between the two pins and tack it in place. Stitch the tape down either side and across the bottom to secure gathering tapes at this point. Stitch across the top edge of the tape, leaving cord ends free for gathering up. Stitch two of the rings that come with the tape, one either side of the tape top.

6 Pull up the tape to the required depth of gathers and secure the cords by winding through the rings in a figure of eight. Place the cloth on the table and adjust gathers if necessary. Stitch the fabric flowers in place if desired. Before laundering the cloth, loosen the gathered tape and remove the flowers.

FABRIC FLOWERS

Cut out two shapes for each petal, place right sides together and stitch around curved edges, leaving the inside edge open. Turn right side out, stuff with wadding, turn in inside edge and stitch closed. Topstitch petal lines.

Make centre circle in same way, turn right side out, slipstitch opening and decorate with French knots (see page 80). Attach petals to back of centre circle, gathering the inside edge as you work so that petals curve up at the ends.

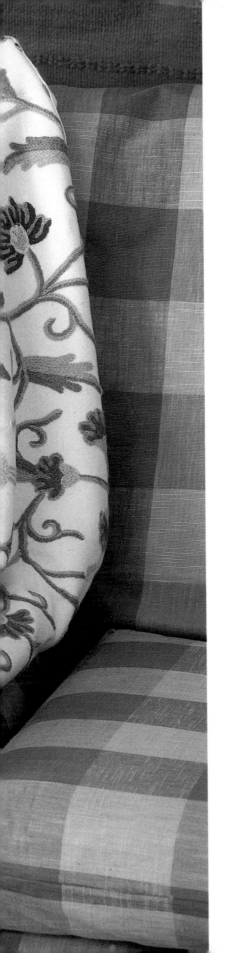

Throws, Rugs and Wall Hangings

Using a throw, casually or carefully arranged, over a fireside chair or sofa is the quick and easy way to give out-of-date, damaged or mismatching upholstery a new lease of life.

Rugs can be used in much the same way, to cover an unattractive or worn floor covering and provide a decorative focus for a room. Plain or patterned fabrics leftover from your sewing projects can be easily transformed into an attractive rug.

Matching wall hangings, placed either side of a door, fireplace or window, create a festive touch at any time of the year. Alternatively, choose a fabric with a simple, bold motif to make a wall hanging that doubles as a playmat for a baby's room.

Step-by-step instructions for making a selection of throws, rugs and wall hangings are covered in this chapter.

Double-sided throw

A double thickness, double-sided throw adds a contemporary touch. It is very versatile, as it can be changed from side to side to match your mood or a room scheme. A throw of this size has many uses – as a chair throw, a bed throw, a car rug or even as a picnic rug.

This throw uses two co-ordinating fabrics to stunning effect. One square is cut larger than the other and the extra fabric is folded round to the opposite side to create a border design. Cord hides any stitching on the reverse side and adds a decorative finish.

Fine wools and similar woven fabrics, velvet or chenille are all ideal for this throw.

MATERIALS:
Soft wool or woven fabric in two colourways, matching thread, cord or braid

FABRIC:
Two squares of fabric, one square the size of the finished throw and the other 20cm (8in) larger, plus braid for the border. The size of the finished throw shown is 117cm (46in). For this you will need a square of fabric this size and a square of fabric 137cm (54in). For the braid you will need 2.1m (2½yd)

1 Cut one square of fabric 117cm x 117cm (46in x 46in) for the bordered side and one piece of fabric 137cm x 137cm (54in x 54in) for the plain side. On the larger square turn under a single 1.25cm (½in) hem to the wrong side and tack down.

2 With wrong sides facing, place the smaller square centrally on the larger one. Pin in position and check that the border is equal on all sides. Tack the two squares together, stitching close to the raw edges of the smaller square.

3 To make the border corners, fold the border around the edge of the top fabric and press in position. At the corners, pin the two side lengths together diagonally to create a mitre (see page 83). Trim the fabric 1.25cm (½in) outside the pin line at each corner. Then turn the border to the wrong side, tack mitred edges together and stitch.

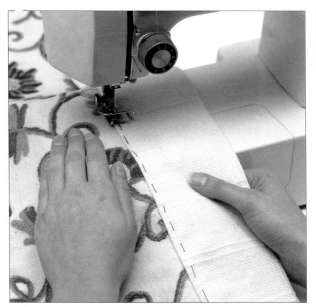

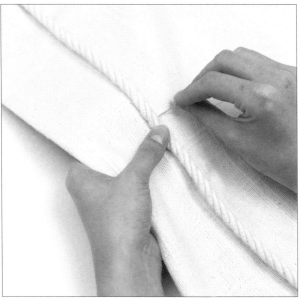

4 Reposition the border back to the right side, with the mitre stitching inside, tack together, then topstitch the border in place. For a neat finish, stitch close to the edge of the tacked hem.

5 To add the braid, turn the throw, reverse side up, and hide stitchline by tacking, then slipstitching, a border line of cord or braid (see pages 84-85) over the machine stitches.

FABRIC CHOICES
For the reverse side of the throw choose a fabric of a similar weight to the top fabric, making sure that it can be cleaned in the same way. Similarly, ensure that any braid or trimming that you use is pre-shrunk and can also be cleaned in the same way as the main fabrics.

Plain fabrics are a good choice for the reverse side of a patterned throw, particularly if the colour echoes one of those used in the patterned fabric.

Cover-up throw

An all-enveloping throw and easy wrap-around cushion covers are a quick and simple alternative to making fitted covers for an old sofa. The covered cushions serve a practical purpose, helping to keep the throw in position. If you prefer not to cover the cushions, make the throw to go over them and tuck it in well.

To measure the sofa, remove the cushions and measure from the floor at the back to the floor at the front, following the sofa's curves. Add 10cm (4in) for hems front and back and allow 20cm (8in) for tuck-in along the back of the seat. Then measure from side to side in the same way, allowing for hems and tuck-in at either side of the seat.

MATERIALS:
Medium-weight furnishing fabric, matching threads, zips

FABRIC:
Main cover: To calculate the length of fabric required, first measure the sofa from front to back and from side to side. Then work out how many widths of fabric you will need by dividing the fabric width measurement into the side-to-side measurement. Then multiply the number of fabric widths by the front to back measurement.
Cushion covers: To calculate the length of fabric required for each cushion, measure around the top and bottom of the cushion from the centre of the back gusset. To calculate the width required, measure from the centre of one side gusset strip to the centre of the opposite one. Add seam allowances to both measurements. You will also need a zip for each cover that is about 2-4cm (1-2in) shorter than its width.

1 Mark and cut out the necessary number of fabric widths to make up the full throw width, matching up any design on the fabric across the widths. When joining widths of patterned fabric, place widths side by side with right side up and tack together using ladder stitch (see page 78) to ensure an accurate pattern match across the seams. If using plain fabric, tack on the back as normal. Stitch with flat fell seams (see page 81), then press.

2 Remove cushions and place cover over sofa, wrong side out. Tuck the throw in at the sofa sides and back, then mark the hem length, checking measurements at the centre of each side and at centre front and back. Pin up a straight double hem to this level. Corners will drape at present. Stitch hems, mitring corners (see page 83) and press throw.

3 To check the effect, replace throw on sofa, right side up and tuck in allowances, continuing the side tucks up and over back and down to front edges and the horizontal back pleat over the arms. As an alternative to draped ends, pick up back and front corners and tie in a decorative knot at the centre of each outer arm.

SIMPLE CUSHION COVERS

Cut out one piece of fabric for each cushion, following the measurements you have taken and matching any motifs to those on the main throw. Turn under a seam allowance along the short ends and insert a zip in this seam (see page 87). Fold the fabric in half across the width, right sides together. Stitch along the two side seams. Press. For neat corners, place cover over cushion, wrong side out and pin a mitre across each corner (see page 83), then stitch. Turn right side out and fit.

Plaited rag rug

This rag rug is made from strips of fabric plaited together. The continuous plait is then stitched to the adjoining length to form a thick rug. It is easy to match up a rug to a room's colour scheme if you use fabric lengths left over from other soft furnishings in the room. However, to obtain an even result it is important to use fabrics of the same weight.

The softly angled corners of the rug are created by plaiting only two of the three strips at the corners. This makes the outside edge wider than the inside, forming the corner shape.

MATERIALS:
Medium to heavyweight furnishing fabric in three colourways, matching quilting thread, card, pencil, metre or yard rule

FABRIC:
The rug shown was made from finished strips 4cm (1⅝in) wide folded from strips of fabric 10cm (4in) wide. To estimate the fabric quantity, cut out three strips and plait up a sample length. Measure the finished plait length and use that measurement to calculate the number of strips and the quantity of fabric. To keep the folded strips even, cut a card rectangle the same width as the unfolded strips.

1 Make a template 10cm (4in) wide from a piece of card. Use this to mark out strips across the fabric. Draw in parallel lines across the fabric, this distance apart, and cut out strips. To avoid having the joins on each strip in the same place on the plait, vary the length of the first cut strips by 10cm (4in).

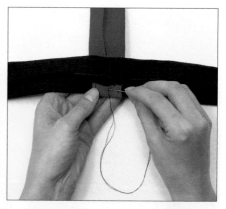

EXCLUDING RAW EDGES
The easiest way to avoid raw edges showing on the rug front is to press the edges to the back as step 2. To conceal them on the rug back, tuck the centre back raw edges in with your finger as you plait.

2 On the card, mark one notch 4cm (1⅝in) from the edge and a second notch 2cm (¾in) beyond this. Fold in the raw edge of one of the strips using the first notch as a guideline. Press in place. Then using the second notch in the card for guidance, fold in a narrower strip along the opposite raw edge to the centre back. Repeat for all the strips.

3 Unfold one end on two of the strips and with right sides facing, hand or machine stitch together along the short raw edge. Refold joined strips as one long length. With wrong side up, lay out third strip, then position long strip, wrong side up, over it to form a T-shape with join at centre. Fold the end of the short strip to the back of the joined strips and stitch to hold.

4 Pin the joining point of the strips to a board and start to plait. In this case, green over red, blue over green and finally red over blue. Do not plait tightly but allow strips to lie flat. To make plaiting easier, roll up the separate lengths and secure each with an elastic band.

5 When the plait is 30cm (12in) long, turn the corner. To do this, leave the inside strip on one side and fold the other two over each other twice. Twist the plait back on itself, press the outer strips in position on the corner with your fingers to neaten the shape, then continue plaiting.

6 To stitch the plaited strips together use quilting thread and ladder stitch (see page 79). Do not pull the thread tight but allow the plaits to lie flat next to one another.

7 To join in further strips, simply unfold the end of the strip, place a strip of the same colour over the end of the first, with right sides together. Machine or hand stitch across the short edge 1.25cm (½in) from the end, turn right side out and refold.

8 Continue plaiting, turning corners and joining strips until the rug reaches the finished size you require. To finish off, trim each strip to a taper and stitch each taper in turn under a loop of the outside plait.

Child's playmat

The delightful design on this fabric has been used to full advantage for this baby's play mat that doubles as a wall hanging. Choose a fabric with simple, bold motifs that are easy to cut around.

Animal shapes on this fabric have been cut out and stuffed to form small toys. Attached with ribbon, some slip neatly into a matching animal pocket while others are fixed in place with touch and close fastening tabs, making the mat a fascinating playtime diversion as well as a comfortable play area.

MATERIALS:

Closely woven cotton furnishing fabric, plain matching lining fabric, heavyweight wadding, narrow ribbon, touch and close fastening tabs, matching sewing threads, tailor's chalk or cloth marker, straight edge

FABRIC:

The finished playmat is 120 x 80cm (47in x 31½in). You will need two pieces of fabric (or one of fabric and one of lining) 122 x 82.5 (48in x 32½in) plus one piece of wadding of the same size. You will need extra fabric, lining and wadding for animals and fabric rectangles for pockets. For each shape that slots into a pocket you will need a length of ribbon 23cm (9in) long. For other animals allow a touch and close fastening tab.

1 Following the sizes given above, cut two rectangles of fabric for the front and back of the mat and one rectangle, the same size, of wadding. Use the tailor's chalk and the straight edge to mark the border line on the rectangle for the top side of the mat, taking it along all four sides of the mat 10cm (4in) inside the outer stitching line.

2 Choose the shapes you want to use for the toys and cut them out, allowing an extra 1.25cm (½in) all round for seam allowance. For each toy that slots into a pocket cut out a rectangle of the same design, allowing space for the toy to slip inside, plus seam allowance. Cut ribbon into 23cm (9in) lengths, allowing one length for each pocket.

3 For each pocket, turn in a single 1.25cm (½in) hem along the sides and base and tack in place. On the top edge, turn under a double 1.25cm (½in) hem and stitch. Pin pockets on the right side of the top piece of the mat, matching up the design. Do not position over the border line or too close to the centre. Tack, then stitch pockets in place.

4 To make the stuffed animals, cut out one motif for each animal. Allow 1.25cm (½in) seam allowance on all sides. Do not try to follow the shape exactly but allow extra fabric around detailed outlines. Place a motif wrong side up on the lining and cut out a matching shape. Right sides together, stitch each motif and matching lining piece together, leaving a 5cm (2in) opening along one edge. Clip into curves, press and turn right side out. Using a round ended object push wadding into the shape until well padded. Place one end of one ribbon length inside the opening of each animal that fits into a pocket and slipstitch opening closed. Omit ribbon for animals attached with touch and close fastening but stitch the top section of the fastening to the back.

6 To attach the animals, turn under the opposite end of the ribbon attached to an animal and slipstitch firmly inside the matching pocket. Decide on positions for other animal shapes and stitch a corresponding touch and close tab to each position on the mat. Do not leave a baby unattended on this mat.

5 To make up the play mat, with right sides facing, place playmat top side rectangle over matching back side rectangle and tack together to hold. Tack wadding rectangle over the top, then stitch around the edge, leaving a 20cm (8in) opening along one side edge. Remove tacking, press mat and trim wadding. Clip corners, turn right side out and slipstitch opening closed. Tack along the border line through all thicknesses, then topstitch through all layers. Remove tacking.

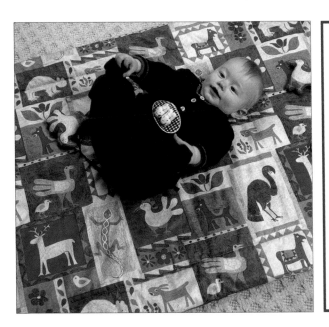

HANGING THE MAT

To hang the mat, attach loops along the top edge and slot through a pole fixed to the wall at play height. Do not use as a quilt.

Quilted wall hanging ✂

This hanging uses large and small motifs cut from a fabric panel. Each shape is backed by a mirror image from the design and sandwiched with wadding. The motifs are arranged down strips of ribbon to complete the design. The large motifs are made around the ribbon rather than attached to it, while the small motifs are stuck in place.

If the fabric you choose does not include mirror images of the motifs or is particularly expensive, then back the shapes with plain lining fabric.

MATERIALS
Furnishing fabric with bold motifs, lining fabric (if mirror-image motifs are not included in the design), lightweight wadding, ribbon, matching sewing threads, glitter fabric paint

FABRIC:
You will need a piece of fabric that includes enough full motifs for each hanging, plus a mirror image of each. Alternatively, buy enough fabric for single motifs and purchase lining for the backs. For one hanging you will need two pieces of ribbon 4cm (1⅝in) wide by the length of the hanging plus seam allowance of 2.5cm (1in) and a piece 42cm (16½in for a bow). You will need the same amount of wadding as fabric.

1 To create the basis for the hanging, cut two lengths of ribbon, the length of the hanging, plus 2.5cm (1in) with one 5cm (2in) shorter than the other. Cut a notch in each at the lower end. Turn under a double 1.25cm (½in) hem across the top of each and slipstitch in place. Use the remaining length of ribbon to create a bow for the top of the hanging.

2 Choose one large and one small motif to use from the design. Use groups of motifs as one shape, as well as single designs. Press the fabric well, then cut out one example of each motif, allowing at least

2cm (¾in) around each. Do not try to follow a complicated outline exactly. With right sides together, pin a motif to its mirror image, carefully lining up the outlines. Cut out the second shape following the cut out outline of the first. If you have no mirror images, cut out the second shape in lining fabric. Also cut out one of each smaller shape from wadding and two of each larger shape from wadding. Repeat until you have cut out all the motifs required for the hanging.

3 To prepare small motifs, pin sets of shapes together, sandwiching the wadding between. Check that the back and front outlines match exactly and pin in position. Knot the end of some tacking thread and working from the centre tack out to each corner to secure the pieces. Use extra tacking lines where necessary. Using a large straight machine stitch, stitch along lines in the design such as leaf veins or flower petal centres.

4 To stitch the small motifs set your sewing machine to do satin stitch and use thread to match the background colour. Satin stitch around the motif or set of motifs. Do not attempt to keep exactly to a complicated outline but curve around the shapes. When you have finished stitching the motif remove the tacking and cut out through all layers close to the stitched outline.

5 Place the two lengths of ribbon side by side with a 5mm (¼in) space between and with the top side uppermost. Position the first large motif, with one wadding shape behind it, over the ribbons near the top, and pin in position. Turn the hanging over and place second wadding shape and mirror image over the back, carefully matching up the outlines with those on the opposite side. Pin, then tack in position (see step 3). Straight stitch along any lines or curves in the design you want to stand out and then satin stitch all layers together around the edge. Trim the edges of the motif, being careful not to cut into the ribbon.

6 Stitch the remaining large motifs in the same way, ensuring that there is enough space to attach the small motifs between them. To complete the design, pin the small motifs in position and check the effect. When you are satisfied with the arrangement, the motifs can either be glued to the ribbon using fabric adhesive or stitched in place where appropriate following leaf vein or flower petal lines. Attach bow and hang using a short rod and cord or a large ring.

ADDING HIGHLIGHTS
Use fabric glitter paint to add highlights to the design. Follow the manufacturer's instructions for applying.

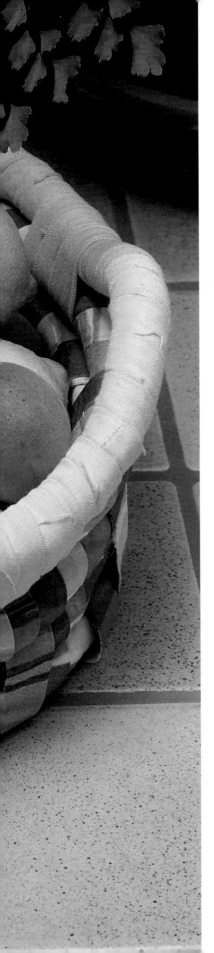

Storage and Screens

Curtains and panels are a decorative way of hiding the contents of a glass-fronted cupboard or open clothes storage. Where narrow alcoves are used for storage, curtains can be used to conceal the area whilst creating a softly draped look for stark walls.

Fabric-covered screens are ideal for concealing an empty fireplace during the summer, or any other less-than-attractive area in your home. Screens are particularly effective when they use a single stunning motif.

Fabric can also be used to create a variety of different types of simple storage. This chapter includes a project for a rope basket covered with fabric strips, which is ideal for use in either a kitchen, bedroom or bathroom.

Cupboard curtains

Glass-fronted cupboards may not always contain items that you wish to show. If you prefer to hide the contents, give cupboards a whole new decorative finish with curtains fixed to the inside of the doors.

These curtains are made with a casing that takes a rod or stretched curtain wire at both top and bottom edges. So that the decorative effect is maintained when the doors are opened a frilled edging is included. Before starting, check that there is room to hang a curtain between the cupboard doors and the interior shelves.

MATERIALS:
Fine to medium-weight furnishing fabric, matching thread, curtain wires or rods

FABRIC:
Fix the curtain wires or rods out of sight above and below as well as out to the sides of the glass. To work out fabric quantities, measure the distance from top to bottom rods and add twice the rod thickness plus 1.25cm (1/2in) for two rod casings and for heading frills top and bottom add 5-10cm (2-4in). Allow 2.5cm (1in) for seam allowance. For the width, measure rod or stretched wire length and multiply by two or three times for the curtain width. Transparent or fine fabrics like voile, net, lace and muslin look best gathered up to three times the width of the rail but allow a width twice the length of the rail for thicker materials. Add 2.5cm (1in) for narrow side hems.

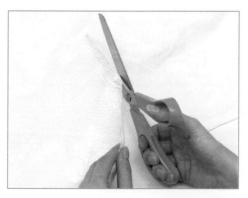

1 Cut out fabric to the required size. If you need to join fabric widths, use narrow French seams (see page 81) and match up any design across the widths.

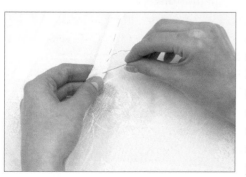

2 For side hems, turn in a narrow double hem along each side of the curtain. Tack to secure and then machine stitch in place. Press.

3 Fold over a narrow single hem along the top edge of the curtain and pin. Add the measurements for the casing and edging frill together, then fold over the pinned edge to this depth. Pin to secure, then stitch along the hem edge. Repeat for the bottom hem.

4 To make the rod casing, measure the casing depth, ie rod thickness plus 5mm (¼in), from the hem edge. Using tailor's chalk, draw a parallel line at this depth along the hem edge. Pin double thickness of fabric together, tack and then stitch along marked line. Press curtain.

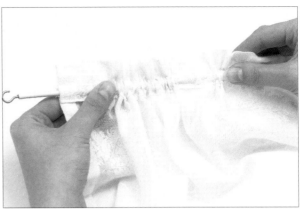

5 To hang the curtain, thread the length of wire or rod through each casing. Adjust the curtain gathers so that they are even along the length and then hang the curtain in the cupboard.

FLAT FABRIC PANEL

A beautiful design that would be lost in the gathers of a curtain can be displayed flat. For this double-sided panel no heading frills are included.

Measure the distance from top to bottom rods and add rod thickness plus 2.5cm (1in). Cut two pieces of fabric this depth, by the rod length plus seam allowances. Place fabric pieces, with right sides together, and stitch along top and bottom edges. Press and turn right side out. Turn in side raw edges and slipstitch closed leaving a space for the rods at top and lower edges. Stitch across the panel, parallel with top and bottom edges to make the rod casings. Hang the panel.

Fabric fire screen

A simple base of medium density fibreboard (MDF) cut to size can be covered with fabric to create an attractive, individual fire screen. Here, a single stunning motif has been attached to a fabric background which is then stretched over wadding on the front of the screen. For the best results with appliqué designs like this, choose a background fabric of the same colour as the background of the motif itself.

Decide on the size of screen that you require and make a template from a rectangle of paper, curving the top corners if desired. Enlarge the foot design template (see page 91), by 200% on a photocopier to make it full size. Take both patterns to a DIY shop and ask them to cut the screen and two feet from MDF.

MATERIALS:

Medium-weight furnishing fabric with a large motif, plain furnishing fabric, double-sided bonding material, heavyweight wadding, matching threads, paper for template, MDF base and feet, paint, iron-on adhesive, masking tape, staple gun, handle, braid, glue

FABRIC:

Motif: You will need a rectangle of patterned fabric featuring one complete motif with at least 5cm (2in) around it and a rectangle of bonding material 1.25cm (½in) smaller than the fabric rectangle on all sides.
Screen: You will need two rectangles of plain fabric the size of the screen, plus 5cm (2in) on all sides and enough wadding and iron-on adhesive to cover one side of the screen.

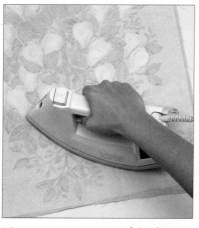

1 First press the patterned fabric well, then cut out a rectangle around the motif to be used. Cut well outside the design, allowing a minimum of 5cm (2in) space around it.

Then cut a rectangle of double-sided bonding material 1.25cm (½in) smaller than the fabric rectangle on all sides. Centre this, with the rough adhesive side down, over the back of the fabric and press on a wool setting, allowing about three to four seconds contact so that the adhesive on the paper is transferred to the fabric.

2 Allowing 1.25cm (½in) outside the design, cut out the motif. Cut in curves around complicated outlines, do not attempt to follow them exactly. Using a dressmaker's pencil, mark the motif centre at top and bottom. Then cut out one piece of background fabric to size of screen plus 5cm (2in) on all sides. With right side outside, press this in half down the length to define the centre. Remove backing paper from the motif, line up marks on the motif with the centre line of the background, then press it in place.

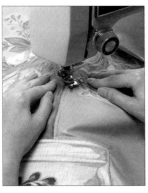

3 To attach the motif to the background, use a close zigzag stitch on the machine and follow the curved outline around the motif to stitch it to the background. Stitch over the cut edge to avoid fraying in the future.

4 Use the screen template to cut out the fabric for the back of the screen, allowing 10cm (4in) extra on all sides. Cut out the iron-on adhesive to the template size. With paper side of adhesive uppermost, centre this over the back of the fabric and press in place using a very low heat. Once it is cool, remove backing and place fabric over back of screen and press again to activate adhesive. Finish by stapling fabric to screen along all the edges, then trim fabric to fit.

5 Cover the front of the screen with wadding, fixing it to the edges with masking tape. Mark the centre of the screen top and bottom, then with the dressmaker's pencil mark the centre of the fabric front piece. Line up marks, then staple to hold the fabric. Gently smooth the fabric to either side and staple at centre side edges. Then staple at 5cm (2in) intervals, smoothing rather than stretching fabric into place. Add further staples, paying particular attention to curved corners. Trim any extra fabric.

6 To neaten the edges, glue braid around the screen to cover the raw edges of the fabric. Turn under the braid edge at the starting and finishing points. Screw the handle in place. Paint the feet to match the screen background colour then fix them to the screen. Highlight the design with fabric glitter paint if desired.

Narrow alcove storage ✂

In a room where space is at a premium, hang clothes from hooks across the alcove width and make a generous floor-length curtain to hide the paraphernalia. This curtain is quickly and easily made from two flat bed sheets sewn together to form a matching curtain and lining. The top frilled valance edge is made by placing the heading tape parallel to the top edge but about 28cm (11in) below it and then allowing the decorated edge of the lining sheet to fall forward and be displayed.

MATERIALS:
Plastic-coated hanging rail, fixing ends and split rings, flat sheets, 8cm (3in) wide curtain heading tape, matching threads, cord tidy

FABRIC:
Use two sheets per curtain and choose sheet size according to the width of the curtain you require. Single sheets make one 180cm (72in) wide curtain to fit a 132cm (52in) alcove.

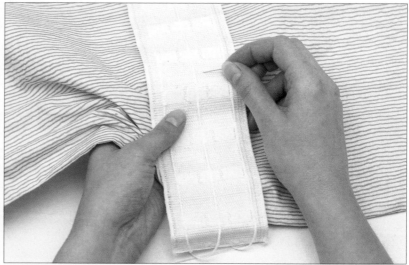

1 To join the sheets, place one on top of the other with right sides together. Pin and then tack to hold. Stitch 1.25cm (½in) from sheet side hems. Press and turn right side out.

2 Decide on the depth required for the frilled valance, then using tailor's chalk draw a line across the wrong side of the fabric at this depth. Cut a length of heading tape the width of the curtain plus 2.5cm (1in). Position the top edge of the tape on the chalk line, leaving 1.25cm (½in) of tape overlapping the side edges, then pin the tape in place. On the leading edge of the curtain secure the tape cords to the back of the tape, then turn the overlap under and pin to the curtain. At the opposite end, pull the cords to the right side ready for gathering, then turn the overlap under and pin in position. Tack the tape in place.

HANGING THE CURTAIN

Buy a rod to fit the width of the alcove plus end pieces and allow enough curtain rings to place them about every 15cm (6in) along the curtain edge.

Measure the length of the curtain from the top of the heading tape to the bottom of the curtain and position the rod at this height up from the floor or slightly lower if you want the curtain to drape on the floor. Fix the end sockets in place on the end walls with the notches to take the rail on the upper side.

To hang the rail, place an end socket cover on the rail first, then thread on the split rings and finally the second socket cover. Place the rail in the socket notches and push each covering in place over a socket.

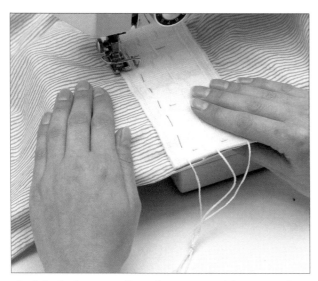

3 Stitch the tape, first along top and bottom edges following the marked line on the tape, and then down each short side edge. Stitch through the cords at the leading edge to secure them, but at the other end stitch beyond the cords. Pull up the cords to gather the curtain to the correct width, tie and wind surplus cord on to a cord tidy. Smooth the valance frill edge towards the front of the curtain and position the split rings at equally spaced intervals along the heading tape.

INSTANT TIEBACK TRICKS

As alternatives to the tassel shown, use a shell necklace, slotting it over a cup hook screwed to the wall, wide ribbon tied in a giant bow, or embroidery silks rolled together (see Tassel tieback, pages 28-29) to form a cord.

Fabric-bound basket

Leftover fabric, cut into strips and wound around coils of rope, forms softly shaped baskets that can be made in a range of sizes and used to hold a wide choice of items from fruit to bathroom accessories. The baskets, made from one long length of rope, are tough but malleable and can be eased into shape.

MATERIALS:
Furnishing fabrics, marine rope, tapestry needle, matching threads

FABRIC:
For a basket 33cm (13in) in diameter and 9cm (3½in) high, you will need 25 strips the fabric width by 4cm (1⅝in) deep and just over 6m (6¾yd) of 2cm (¾in) thick, fairly stiff rope.

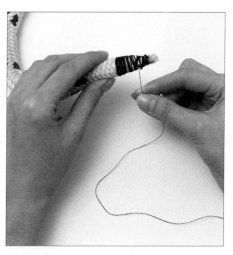

1 Using scissors, taper the end of the length of rope so that it comes to a point. Wrap thread around the cut end to hold. Starting about 10cm (4in) from this end, begin to wind the first strip of fabric around the rope back towards the point.

2 On reaching the pointed rope end, bend the point around it to form a loop and tightly wrap the fabric around it to form the central coil. Continue wrapping the fabric strip around the rope, while spiralling the rope around the central coil.

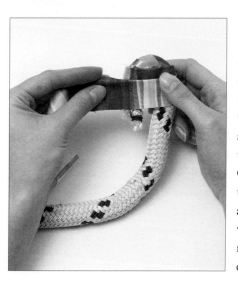

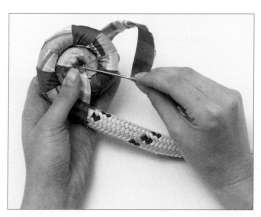

3 To lace the coils together, thread the strip end on to a tapestry needle and pass it through the central loop. On later coils, push it through the gap between the previous coil and the one before that. Fix in this way about every four to five turns of the fabric strip.

AVOIDING FRAYED EDGES
To avoid frayed edges, fold under the left-hand edge of the strip as you work. The right-hand edge is hidden under the next strip. After completing a lacing strip tuck in any raw edges still showing with the outside edge of some small scissors.

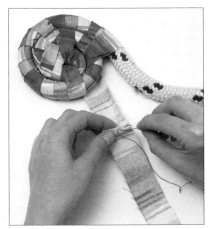

4 To attach fabric strips, when you reach the end of the first strip, place second strip over the first, with right sides facing, and stitch together across the end. Continue as before.

5 When the base is the required size, start to make the sides by laying the next coil so that it overlaps the one before, lacing them together in this position. Continue in the same way, forming the sides of the basket, until it is the desired height.

6 To form the first handle, secure the top coil to the one before it, three times in succession. Wrap the fabric around the rope about nine times, then bend to form a handle shape and fix to the coil below three times as before. Make the opposite handle in the same way.

7 To finish off, taper the end of the rope (see step 1) then wind fabric over the taper and previous coil tightly to secure, turn in the end of the fabric strip and stitch in place inside the basket rim.

Lampshades

Lampshades can be quite easy and quick to make. With adhesives, stiffeners and adhesive-backed ribbons providing a simple method, you can achieve an impressive result. Making your own shade considerably widens the choice of colours and patterns you have available and allows you to complement the furnishings in a room perfectly.

Most fine or medium-weight furnishing fabrics are suitable and cotton and linen are ideal.

For an even quicker, individual effect, you can add decoration to an existing plain shade, tailoring it perfectly to the room scheme.

Choosing shades and bases

Table lamps form part of a room's decorative effect as well as providing a light source. According to their shape and their position, table lamps may create atmospheric background light, while still lighting the whole room, or they may spread only enough light to enable you to perform tasks like writing, sewing or reading. Coolie shape shades allow a spread of light but need to be positioned high enough for the light to fall on a working area.

Consider position and shape, according to the type of light you wish to create. An alternative choice is a shade hung low over a table on a long flex from the ceiling. A large shade works better in this situation.

BALANCING BASE AND SHADE

The colour, shape and material of the base and shade look better if they complement each other. Before choosing a shade size and shape, look at complete shades and bases to see how they have been matched up and what effect you most like.

SHADE DECORATION

Though a plain shade can look pretty, adding simple decorations creates an individual effect to complement a specific room scheme. By using fabric adhesive to stick materials in place or clear adhesive for most other materials you can attach unusual decorative objects to a plain shade.

▲ This well matched shade and base have a simple elegance that requires no further adornment.

▲ Coiled rope and a scalloped shell form a simple nautical design on a plain shade.

▲ Using pinking shears, cut out a series of small triangles or squares from check or striped fabric, then stick to the shade front in a group to form a patchwork effect. Alternatively cut out a series of small triangles, overlap them slightly and fix them around the lower edge to form a zigzag border.

▲ Wire-edged ribbon can be used to create a giant bow with curling tails falling to the shade's lower edge. Or, tie narrow ribbon around the side of the shade, making a neat bow. Another use of ribbon is to lace around the top and bottom edge with ribbon or glittery gold or silver cord. Use a hole punch and make evenly spaced holes.

Coolie shade

The sleek lines of a coolie shade add style to a room's decoration and act as an ideal basis for decorative trimmings. An inexpensive shade can be transformed with a new fabric covering and some extra decorative touches.

The fabric is fixed with spray adhesive to cover the old coolie shade. Always follow the manufacturer's instructions when using spray adhesive. It should not be inhaled, so wear a mask and work in a well ventilated area.

MATERIALS:
Coolie shade, fine or medium-weight furnishing fabric, brown paper for pattern, double-sided adhesive tape, repositionable spray adhesive, fabric adhesive, ribbon for decoration

FABRIC:
Make a pattern from brown paper (see step 1 below) and measure this for the quantity of fabric required. Place with the central fold line on the pattern lined up with the fabric straight grain. Measure at the widest points, and allow 2cm (¾in) seam allowance on all sides.

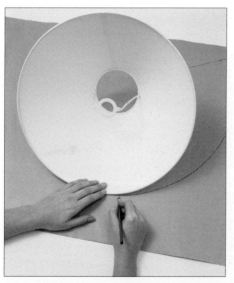

1 To make the pattern, draw a straight line on the brown paper, close to one long edge and at an angle. Lay the shade over this, matching the line on the paper to the seam on the shade. Carefully roll the shade round on the paper, marking top and bottom edges as you go. When you reach the seam again, stop and draw in a second straight line between top and bottom curved lines. Add a parallel line outside one straight line and 4cm (1⅝in) from it for the seam allowance. Cut out the pattern, lay over the shade to check and adjust if necessary. Fold in half.

2 Place the fabric right side up and position the pattern on it, ensuring that the central fold line goes through a central motif on the fabric or follows the straight grain. Pin in place and cut out the fabric shape adding a 2cm (¾in) allowance along top and base edges.

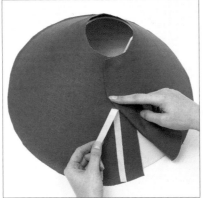

3 Fix a length of double-sided adhesive tape along the seam edge of the shade. Spray the shade all over with spray adhesive, then stick one edge of the fabric to the adhesive strip, making sure that allowances top and bottom are equal. Smooth the fabric in place, keeping allowances even.

4 To attach the other end of the fabric to the shade, fix a length of double-sided adhesive tape to the fabric 3.5cm (1½in) from the start point. Peel off the protective strip on the tape, turn under an allowance of 1cm (½in) on the raw fabric edge and stick fabric down on to the tape.

5 Turn the raw edges on the top edge to the back of the shade and fix in place with fabric adhesive. Snip into the fabric where necessary to ensure it lies flat on the wrong side and hold in place with clothes pegs until the adhesive is dry. Repeat along the lower edge.

6 To decorate the frame, cut four lengths of ribbon to fit around the shade from top to bottom, adding 60cm (24in) to each length for bows. Position either side of the centre front and centre back and tie in place with bows.

Pleated fabric shade

Pleated fabric shades fit neatly into most room schemes and can be made in a wide range of shapes and sizes. They can be created from leftover lengths of fabric used for other soft furnishings in the room or from fabrics that add colour and sparkle to otherwise spartan room schemes.

An added bonus is that they require no sewing skills. The chosen fabric is fused to a heavy-duty fabric stiffener, edged with wired self-adhesive ribbon and then pleated up and fixed to the ring with strong thread and ribbon laced through holes to pull up the shade. The holes are produced with the aid of a standard hole or leather punch.

MATERIALS:
Closely woven furnishing fabric, lampshade ring with fitment, heavyweight iron-on fabric stiffener, pencil and ruler, wired adhesive trimming, hole punch, narrow ribbon, small tassel, fabric adhesive, bodkin, strong thread

FABRIC:
Measure the lower edge of the shade. You will need a rectangle of fabric twice this length by the chosen depth of the shade plus 2cm (¾in) on all sides. Cut the stiffener to the chosen depth and length. For the edging, cut two pieces of fabric adhesive ribbon the same length as the fabric. For the narrow ribbon, measure the ring circumference at the top of the shade and double it.

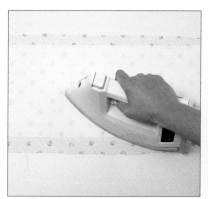

1 First cut out the fabric, making sure that the long edges follow the fabric design or straight grain. Place the stiffener centrally on the wrong side of the fabric rectangle and press to fuse the stiffener to the fabric (see pages 12-13). Once fused, trim off the excess fabric along the edges of the stiffener.

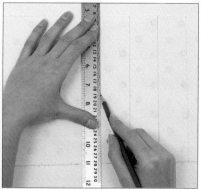

2 With the fabric stiffener side uppermost, make pencil marks at 4cm (1½in) intervals on both long edges. Join up the marks across the width with light pencil lines. Finally, measure 2cm (¾in) from the top edge and draw a line along the length of the fabric at this depth. This is the guideline for the punched holes.

3 Peel off the wider half of the backing paper from one of the lengths of wired adhesive ribbon and, with the centre of the tape on the fabric edge, gently press the ribbon on to the right side of the shade. Peel off the remaining backing strip, fold the ribbon to the wrong side and press firmly. Repeat for the other edge.

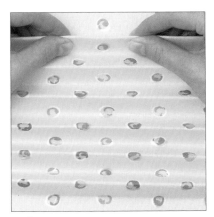

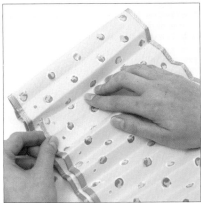

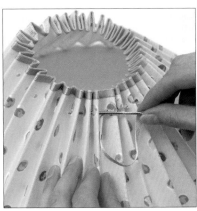

4 Working from the wrong side, crease the fabric along the first marked line. Then fold up to meet the next line and crease in the same way, forming a 2cm (¾in) wide pleat between. Continue to fold and pleat until the far end of the strip is reached. Turn the strip to the right side and firmly pinch in the pleats with your fingers.

5 Following the pencil guideline on the top edge, punch a hole half-way between each pleat. Pull up the shade with some thread to fit the lampshade ring roughly. The pleats should fit comfortably around the ring: if the length is too long shorten it. Remove the temporary thread. Overlap and glue the strip ends together, making the join on an inside pleat.

6 To lace up the shade, thread a bodkin with the narrow ribbon, then starting at the centre front of the shade (the opposite side to the join) take it through the holes and pull up to fit the ring. Knot the ribbon and trim the ends diagonally to prevent them from fraying.

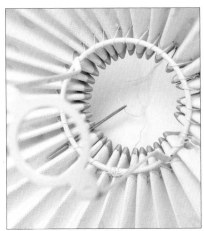

7 Thread the bodkin with strong thread. Knot it to the ribbon on the inside of the shade. Pass the thread round the ring, then under the next section of ribbon. Continue until all of the shade is attached to the ring, then fasten off. Attach the tassel to the ribbon over the knot.

Tools and Techniques

This chapter covers the tools and techniques necessary to create accomplished results time after time. Almost no extra tools are needed for the projects contained in this book, other than those found in most sewing kits, but using the right tools makes the job easier and the result more proficient.

Tried-and-tested sewing techniques are fully explained, showing you exactly how to tackle a particular task, whether it is attaching trimmings, sewing in a zip, or creating a straight-sided corner or a neat curve. Information on securing raw edges, pressing your work and clipping seams helps ensure a professional finish.

A final section on fabric care and cleaning methods gives all the information necessary to ensure the soft furnishings you create continue to look as good as when they were new.

Essential sewing kit

Good quality tools last and make it easier to achieve consistently good results, so choose the best you can afford. A sewing box with compartments is a very useful addition to your sewing kit, keeping everything separate and easy to find.

MEASURING AND MARKING

Tape measure: a vital part of any sewing kit. Choose a tape measure made of nylon or some other material that will not stretch and that has metal protective ends. Each side of the tape should start and finish at opposite ends so that you do not have to unwind the tape to find a starting point.

Metre or yard stick: important for measuring lengths of fabric and for marking straight lines. Make sure that it is straight, has not warped and that the markings appear on both sides.

Steel tape: the most reliable tool for measuring items like furniture or windows when working out quantities of material required.

Dressmaker's carbon paper: useful for transferring designs or other markings from a pattern to fabric. It is used, like other carbon paper, with the shiny side face down on the fabric and the pattern over it.

Tailor's chalk: comes in a range of colours but white is the easiest to remove later. Keep the edge sharp or alternatively use a chalk pencil which has a brush for removing the marks.

Pencil: for copying patterns on to tracing paper. A soft pencil, such as a 2B, is the easiest to use.

CUTTING

Pinking shears: have a serrated blade which makes a zigzag cut. They are used to neaten raw edges, particularly on fabrics that fray easily.

Cutting-out scissors: should have a 15cm (6in) blade and be flat on one side. Never use on any other material except fabric.

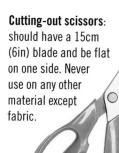

Needlework scissors: are necessary for snipping threads, cutting into or notching seams, making buttonholes and other close trimming jobs.

STITCHING

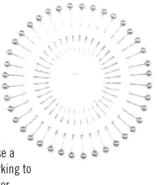

Sewing needles: keep an assortment of needles in your sewing kit. The most useful sizes range from 3-10. The higher the number the finer the needle. Betweens are short, sharp needles that are ideal for fine hemming. Sharps, which are longer and allow more than one stitch on the needle at a time, are useful for tacking or gathering. There is also a wide range of specialist needles available, including a crewel needle with a long eye and a tapestry needle, which has an eye large enough to take narrow ribbon or fabric strips.

Pins: come in a wide range of lengths and thicknesses. Those with glass or plastic heads are the most visible and easiest to use. Use a pin cushion to store pins when working to avoid 'lost and hazardous' pins later.

Threads: mercerised cotton is ideal for stitching cotton or linen. Choose 40 for general use, 50 or 60 for finer fabrics. Core-spun thread, made from polyester with a coating of cotton, is tough, and suitable for use on all but fine fabrics. Use silk thread on silk and wool. Tacking thread breaks easily and is suitable only for tacking. Button hole twist is the best choice for sewing on buttons.

Thimble: protects your fingertip when hand sewing.

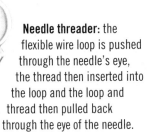

Needle threader: the flexible wire loop is pushed through the needle's eye, the thread then inserted into the loop and the loop and thread then pulled back through the eye of the needle.

MACHINE WORK

Sewing machine: basic machining skills and a sewing machine that does straight stitch, zigzag, buttonholes and reverse, are all that are needed to make the projects in this book.

Machine feet: come in a range of designs for specific jobs. Apart from a standard foot you will find a one-sided zip or piping foot, which can be adjusted to right or left, a very useful asset. A roller foot works well on shiny fabrics, like plastic laminated fabric, and a transparent foot helps you to see detailed work like appliqué clearly.

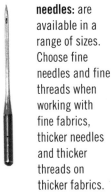

Machine needles: are available in a range of sizes. Choose fine needles and fine threads when working with fine fabrics, thicker needles and thicker threads on thicker fabrics.

Stitches and seams

Specific stitches and certain types of seams are ideal for use in different situations. This guide illustrates the principal hand stitching techniques used in the book, as well as showing the different ways of joining pieces of fabric together.

PREPARING SEAMS AND HEMS

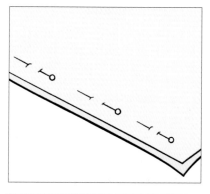

1 Pin fabrics together prior to tacking. On simple joins you can place pins at right angles to the seam and stitch without tacking first.

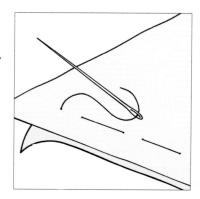

2 Tack adjacent to stitchline on the seam allowance. Use large running stitches which are quick to work and to remove. Place permanent stitches on stitchline.

LADDER STITCH

This is the professional method used to tack two pieces of a patterned fabric together so that the pattern matches across the seam. It is done from the right side of the fabric. You can also use it as a permanent stitch if you take smaller stitches. Ladder stitch also joins the plaits of the rag rug (see pages 50-51).

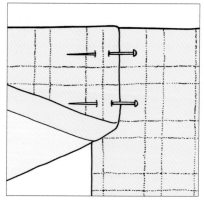

1 On one of the two pieces of fabric to be joined, press under 1.25cm (½in) along the edge. Then place this folded edge, with raw edges matching, over the second piece of fabric. Match pattern and pin in position.

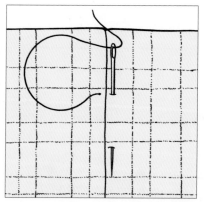

2 Fix the thread within the fold line, then take it straight across to the flat fabric and running directly down the side of the fold, bring the needle out 1.5-2cm (½-¾in) further down the seamline next to the fold.

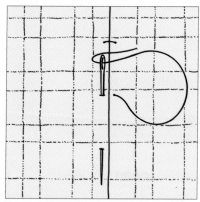

3 Take the needle straight across to the fold and push it down inside the fold edge for another 1.5-2cm (½-¾in). Repeat these two stitches for the length of the seam. Then turn the fabric to the wrong side to stitch it.

HERRINGBONE STITCH

This is the stitch used to hold interlinings in place but it can also be used to fix a raw-edged hem.

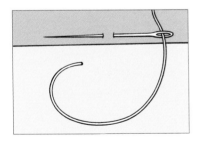

1 Tack the interlining in place to the fabric it is to back. Secure the thread under the interlining and bring the needle up through it, then working from left to right, take the thread diagonally to the main fabric and take a small back stitch of one to two threads only in the main fabric.

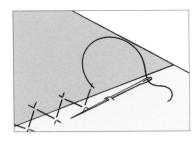

2 Still working diagonally, move across to the interlining and make another small back stitch through the interlining only. Continue in this way to the end and secure the thread in the interlining.

SLIPSTITCHING SEAMS

This is used to join two folded edges together and is used when a gap is left in stitching to turn an item through from the wrong to the right side.

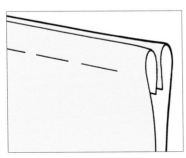

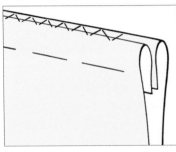

1 Fold under a narrow hem on both pieces of fabric to be joined. Tack to hold folded edges together.

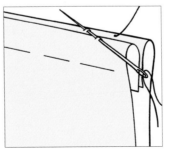

2 Hide the fastened end of the thread within the far hem and then, with folded edges held together, bring the thread into the inner side of the fold of the near hem and take a small stitch. Then take a second small stitch further along in the far hem and pull the thread.

3 Continue in this way until the opening is closed. Do not pull the thread too tight and ensure that stitches and thread are as invisible as possible.

SLIPSTITCHING HEMS

Although machine stitching a hem is quicker, slipstitching creates a neater finish as the stitches are almost invisible on the right side of the fabric.

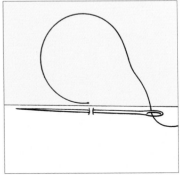

1 Fasten the thread with a knot or backstitch in the fabric of the hem and then bring the needle out on the folded edge of the hem. Pick up one thread, or at the most two, from the main fabric close to the hem edge.

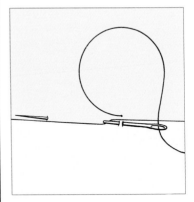

2 Take a long stitch of 2-2.5cm (¾-1in) along the fold of the hem and pull the thread through. Continue in this way, picking up a thread from the main fabric and taking a long stitch, along the hem edge until the hem is stitched.

FRENCH KNOTS

These small surface knots are used for the cat's muzzle on pages 36-37. French knots are often used in embroidery.

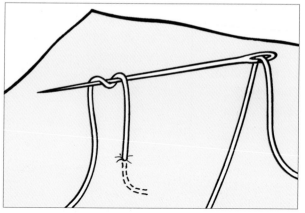

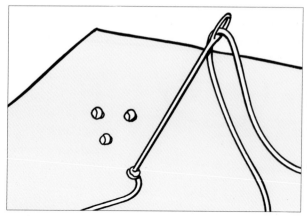

1 Bring thread from back to front, pull taut with one hand while twisting the needle round the thread several times.

2 Reinsert the point of the needle back into the hole where it emerged and pull the thread through to leave a knot on the front surface. Fasten off or go on to the next stitch.

SATIN STITCH

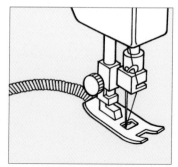

Satin stitch can be done on any swing needle sewing machine. This uses zigzag stitch set so that stitches are wide yet close together. It may appear as a buttonhole stitch on your machine, otherwise set zigzag on a wide measure with stitches close together and do a test, adjusting until you get the best effect.

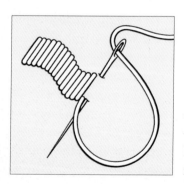

Satin stitch can also be done by hand but this is much more time consuming. Use long, straight stitches and place them close together side by side, keeping the thread flat and even.

GATHERING

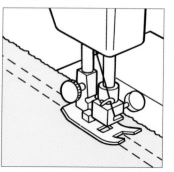

1 For gathering use the longest straight stitch on your sewing machine. The length can be adjusted on your machine's stitch length regulator. It is best to run two lines of stitching next to each other and about 5mm (¼in) apart. When gathers are pulled up the two lines of threads make the final stitching more even.

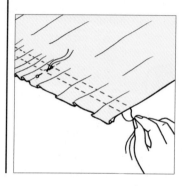

2 Pull up the two lines of threads and check that gathers are even along the length. Work long lengths in separate 60cm (24in) sections. Secure pulled threads around a pin.

FLAT FELL SEAM

The raw edge of a flat fell seam is encased within the seam but, unlike a French seam, both lines of stitching appear on the surface. This makes it a very tough seam which is ideal for use on furnishings like bedding or table linen that are regularly laundered. Here the stitching is done on the back of the fabric but it can also be done on the front.

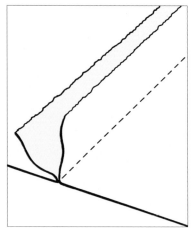

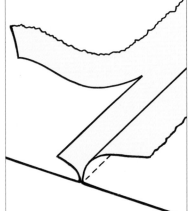

1 With right sides together match up the raw edges of the fabric pieces. Pin, tack and then stitch 1.25cm (½in) from the raw edge.

2 Press to one side. Then trim the seam allowance on the underside of the seam to 5mm (just under ¼in).

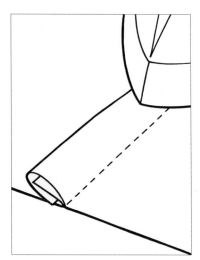

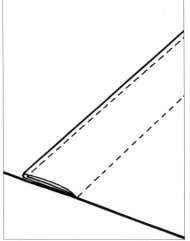

3 Press the wider seam allowance in half with the narrower allowance encased in it. Then press the seam down on to the back of the fabric.

4 Pin the seam in place and tack to hold it secure while you work. Then machine stitch the seam close to the folded edge.

FRENCH SEAMS

A French seam is really two seams, one enclosed within the other. The raw edges are contained within the finished seam giving a tough fray-free finish on the wrong side. It is a neat, narrow seam that is ideal for use on sheer fabrics.

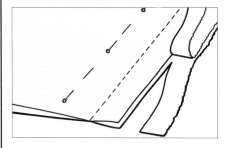

1 With wrong sides together, match raw edges of the pieces of fabric to be joined. Pin, then stitch 5mm (¼in) outside the finished seam line. If necessary, trim close to stitched line.

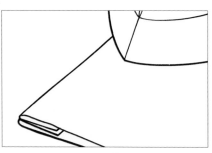

2 Press the seam flat. Turn with right sides of the fabric together and with this first seam line on the edge, press well.

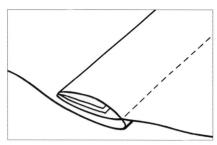

3 Tack, then stitch along the finished seam line. Press.

Curves and corners

Curves and corners need a little extra care, and some special stitching and trimming, if they are to wear well, look good and lie flat.

When stitching a curve, work slowly to ensure the seam allowance remains even and use a shorter stitch than normal to give extra strength.

Mitring a corner neatens it and helps reduce fabric bulk. Mitred corners may be cut or, if the hem might be dropped at a later date, simply folded and stitched.

CURVES

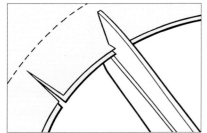 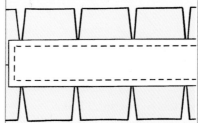 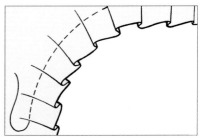

1 Clip the seam allowance at 2.5cm (1in) intervals, cutting to within 3mm (⅛in) of the stitching. Press the seam flat.

2 If part of the seam will get hard wear, strengthen it by stitching a length of narrow seam binding over the seam in this area.

3 On a wide curved hem use gathers to pull up the fabric evenly on the corner, then neaten the edge with bias binding.

STITCHING CORNERS

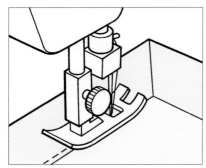 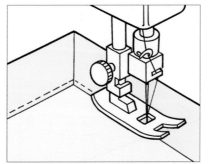 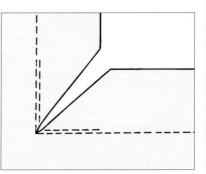

1 To get a sharp angle when stitching a corner, stop one stitch away from the corner and do the last stitch slowly, using the hand wheel if necessary. Leave the needle down in the fabric.

2 Raise the foot and turn the fabric, then lower the foot and continue stitching. To give the corner extra strength use a shorter stitch just before and after the corner.

3 On an inside corner, run a second line of stitching just inside the seam allowance close to the first line for 2.5cm (1in) either side of the corner. Clip the corner so that it lies flat.

MITRING AN EVEN HEMMED CORNER

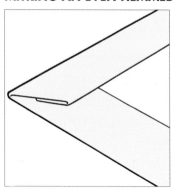

1 On the side and lower edges of the fabric press under a single hem to the wrong side. Then turn under another hem to make a double hem. Press well so that the edge lines of the hems are clear.

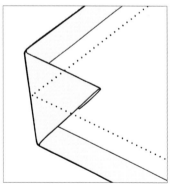

2 Unfold the second part of the hem only. Fold the fabric diagonally, so that the fold runs across the corner point of the finished hem edge. Press this fold, then open out all pressed edges.

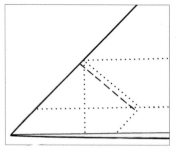

3 With right sides of the fabric facing, fold the fabric at the corner diagonally, with the angled fold lines on top of one another. Tack 5mm (¼in) outside this fold line to the first hem fold line only.

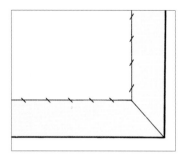

4 Stitch along tacked line, then trim the raw edge to 5mm (¼in), cutting right across the corner. Press seam flat, then turn hem right side out, using a pair of round-ended scissors to push the corner out. Finally, with the hem in place, slipstitch hems.

MITRING AN UNEVEN HEMMED CORNER

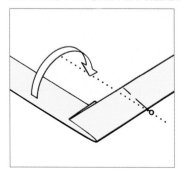

1 Press under a single hem as step 1 above. Press in a double hem on what will be the narrower edge, then mark with a pin where hem edge meets lower pressed hem edge.

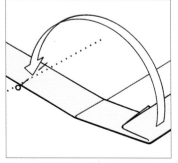

2 Open out and then repeat with the wider hem, marking the point where it meets the narrower hem edge.

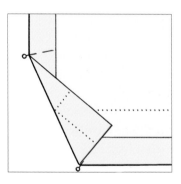

3 Unfold the second part of the hem only and, with single hems in position, press the corner fabric diagonally from one pin mark to the other.

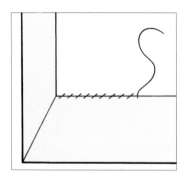

4 Then either trim the corner fabric (see steps 3 and 4 above) or replace the double hems and slipstitch mitred corner without removing corner fabric.

Attaching trimmings

Decorative trimmings may be applied to the edge of fabric or used to decorate its surface. Application methods vary according to the type of trimming and its position. Usually a trimming is added at the final stage of the making up process but some are designed to slot into a seam when it is being stitched.

Match the style, weight and type of trimming to individual projects and ensure that all the elements can be laundered in the same way.

BRAID

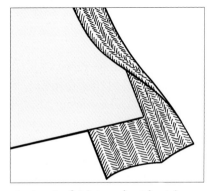

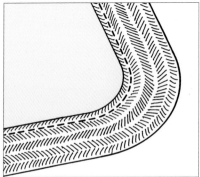

NARROW BRAID

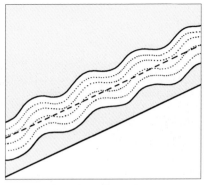

1 Apply fold-over braid with the narrower edge on the fabric's right side, tacking both layers in place through the fabric.

2 Topstitch from the right side close to the edge. This also catches the slightly wider band of braid on the wrong side.

Narrow braid such as ricrac can be attached with a single line of topstitching down the centre.

FRINGE

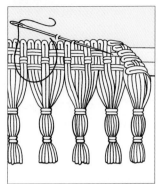

When applying a fringe to the edge of a tablecloth, throw or bedcover, begin by turning a narrow hem to the right side of the fabric. Then tack the fringe braid edge in place over this hem and machine stitch in position.

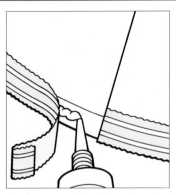

TRIMMING A LAMPSHADE
Apply fabric adhesive to the lampshade edge, following manufacturer's instructions. Cut a piece of braid or fringe, allowing 2.5cm (1in) more than the required length. Fold one raw end under 1.25cm (½in) and, starting from the seam, stick trimming in place round the shade edge. Finish at the far end by turning the raw edge under again to just meet the first fold. Slipstitch folded ends together.

CORD

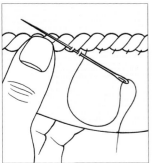

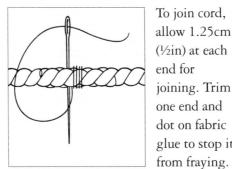

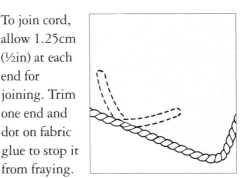

If the cord is not to be attached to the edge of the fabric, mark the line it is to follow first with tailor's chalk or tacking. Stitch cord in place using slipstitch and a thread that matches the background fabric. Use your other hand to hold the cord in position as you work.

To join cord, allow 1.25cm (½in) at each end for joining. Trim one end and dot on fabric glue to stop it from fraying. Allow to dry. Trim the other end, apply a dot of glue to this, then press in place to the end of the first length. Allow glue to dry and slipstitch the new length in position. To disguise the join, cover it with a circle of matching threads.

If the join meets over a seam insert both cord ends in the seam. Close the seam and slipstitch cords together on the top edge to form a continuous line.

RIBBON

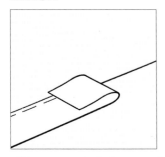

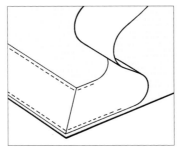

When applying ribbon, first mark where it is to go with tailor's chalk or tacking. Tack the ribbon in place over the marked line. When applying satin ribbon, which shows stitch marks, tack close to the edges. To attach the ribbon, topstitch down each side using straight stitch. Alternatively use zigzag or a decorative embroidery stitch and stitch over the edges of the ribbon.

When applying ribbon along the edge of fabric, turn the hem on the fabric to the wrong side to the width of the ribbon. Line up the ribbon with the hem edge, mitring it at the corners, and machine stitch in place along either side.

LACE

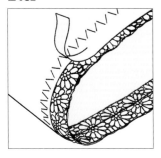

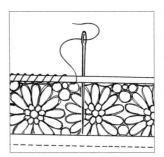

To apply a lace trim, place edging lace, right side up, over the right side of the fabric edge allowing about 1.25cm (½in) overlap. Stitch close to the lace edge using zigzag stitch on the machine. Turn to the wrong side and trim the fabric back to the stitching line, then go over the stitching line again using machine satin stitch.

To create a lace insert first draw a line on the right side of the fabric where the lace is to go. Centre the lace over the line, tack to secure, then topstitch in position close to each edge. Turn to the wrong side and cut away the fabric below the lace leaving 5mm (¼in) along each edge. Roll these fabric edges to the stitching line and oversew to neaten.

Zips and fastenings

Those items which need regular washing must have covers that can be easily removed. Openings can be unobtrusive, as when a zip closes the gap, or obvious, as when brightly coloured buttons and buttonholes are used to create a focal point in the design. Touch and close fastening has many uses, not only for openings in cushions and covers but for attaching fabrics to hard surfaces for tiebacks, pelmets, blinds or a dressing table skirt. Below we show the methods used to attach a range of fastenings.

BUTTONS

As buttons form an obvious method of fastening, use them as a feature, choosing strong colours and designs.

Buttons usually fall into two types. Most have holes in the button's surface for attaching the button but some have a looped stem through which the thread slots. When attaching buttons, start by marking any positions for buttons with tailor's chalk. Use a strong thread and secure the end of the thread with backstitches over the mark.

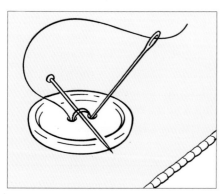

Secure a button with surface holes to the fabric through the holes, then place a pin under the thread and make about ten stitches. Remove the pin, pull the button away from the fabric and wind the thread around the stitches to create a short shank. Stitch into the shank and fabric to finish.

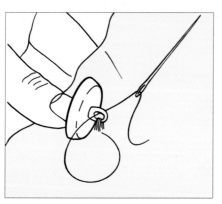

For a button with looped stem, angle the button and make up to ten stitches through the loop and the fabric then secure.

MACHINED BUTTONHOLES

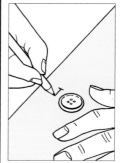

1 Match up with the buttons and mark the position for the buttonholes on the fabric with a fabric pencil or with a double sideways stitch at each end.

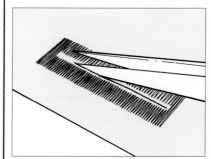

2 Follow the instructions for working a buttonhole in your sewing machine manual. To cut the buttonhole open use a fine bladed craft knife. Place the buttonhole over a cork and start the cut with the blade in the centre of the buttonhole, then finish it off with small sharp-pointed scissors.

ZIPS

This is the best method of inserting a zip in a cushion or cover seam and the result is almost invisible. Fit the zip before the cushion or cover is made up.

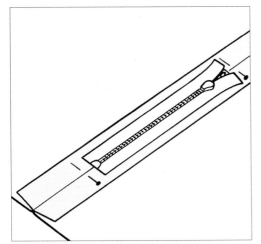

1 Tack the seam, then position the zip centrally in the tacked seam (where the seam remains open at one end and the zip is to be positioned at the end, allow 2.5cm (1in) beyond it for a hook and eye or press studs). Mark with pins the position of the zip allowing an opening 1.25cm (½in) longer than the length of the zip teeth, then stitch the seam at each end up to the pin marks and reverse to secure the ends.

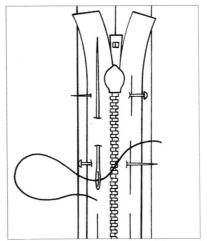

2 Press the seam open, including the tacked area for the zip, and on the wrong side place the zip face down centrally over the tacked area. Pin then tack the zip in position 5mm (¼in) from the teeth down either side and across the ends where the seam stitching ends.

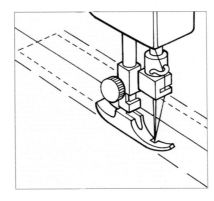

3 Insert a zipper foot in the machine, turn the fabric to the right side and stitch just inside the tacked line along both sides and across the ends. Secure threads. Remove tacking and press, avoiding the zip.

TOUCH AND CLOSE FASTENING

This comes in two sections and either as tape or a range of different sized dots. One section has a mass of soft loops on the surface and the other has tiny hooks. Sections adhere to each other when pushed together. Touch and close fastening with a hook section that can be stuck to a hard surface is also available. This type of fastening is ideal for pelmets and valances as well as many types of window blinds.

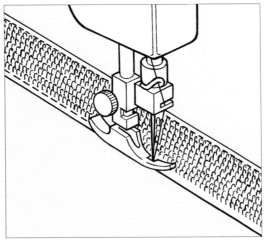

Place the hook section, right side up, on what will be the lower surface. Using the zip foot on the machine, stitch in place around or along the edges. Then slipstitch the loop section, right side up, on the underside of the top surface. Hand stitching ensures that it is unobtrusive.

Finishing

Regular pressing, after every stage of sewing is completed, helps to ensure a professional finish. Have the iron and ironing board set up and ready for use whilst you sew, and if you do not have a steam iron, have a spray bottle to hand to dampen surfaces. Set the iron to the temperature recommended for the fabric and always test it on a scrap of fabric before you start pressing. When pressing from the right side, place a cloth over the fabric to avoid leaving a sheen. Use muslin or a similar lightweight fabric for fine fabrics and a tea towel, kept for the purpose, for other materials.

Neatening the edges of all seam allowances also helps to ensure a long lasting finish, making the finished article as neat on the wrong side as the right. There are several ways to secure raw edges and the most suitable technique will depend on the weight and type of fabric used.

PRESSING SEAMS

1 Press each seam as soon as you have sewn it. Press on the wrong side of the fabric, following the line of stitches. Hold the iron down briefly over one area, before lifting it and transferring it to the next.

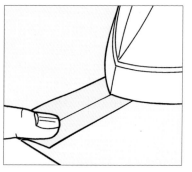

2 After pressing the closed seam, open the allowance and, sliding your fingers down the seam to open it with one hand, follow with the point of the iron to press the seamline open. Finally press down the allowance at either side using the full base of the iron.

PRESSING DELICATE FABRICS

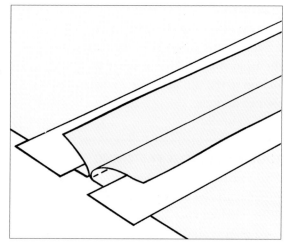

If pressing a seam is likely to leave marks on the right side of the fabric cut thin strips of card and slip these under the seam allowances to protect the fabric, moving them down as you proceed.

Fabrics with a deep pile like velvet are easily crushed when pressed. Press them wrong side up, with a spare piece of fabric, pile side up, underneath. Use steam and a minimum of pressure.

NEATENING SEAMS

To avoid raw edges fraying, it is best to neaten the edges of all seam allowances. There are several ways to secure raw edges and the most suitable technique will depend on the weight and type of fabric used.

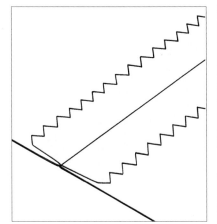

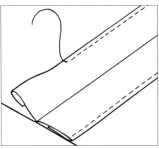

A straight stitched folded edge is a neat method that is ideal for light to medium-weight fabrics that are not bulky.

Turn under allowance edges by about 5mm (¼in) and press. Straight stitch down the sides close to the folded edge to hold it in place.

Pinking is a quick and easy method that is suitable for cottons and fine fabrics that do not fray easily. Simply trim seam allowance edges with pinking shears.

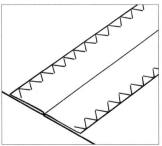

Zigzag edging is the most commonly used method of neatening raw edges and is good for bulky fabrics or those that fray.

With a short, narrow, zigzag stitch, sew down the allowance, slightly in from the edge then trim the edge just short of the stitches. On fabrics that fray badly use a wider stitch.

FABRIC CARE

- Wash items before they become badly soiled and treat stains immediately.
- When removing a stain, never scrub it but, working from the edges, dab at it until the stain disappears. Scrubbing spreads the damage.
- On liquid stains, including wine, cover the area with salt to draw up as much liquid as possible. Then place the item in cold water to soak for half to one hour. Finish by washing in the usual way.
- Tea and coffee stains should be soaked immediately in pre-wash biological powder, then washed in the usual way.
- On fruit and fruit juice stains, rub fabric with salt before soaking in cold water. Rub with neat liquid detergent. Finish by washing in the usual way.
- On solids, scrape off as much as you can using a palette knife before treating the stain.

- On biological stains, such as blood or milk, soak fabric in biological detergent before washing.
- Iron tablecloths flat, do not press in folds and refold in a different way after each washing to avoid well defined crease lines.
- Press embroidery on the wrong side. Do not press lace cloths or mats but instead lay out flat and pin in position, leaving until dry.
- If you are unsure if a fabric is colourfast do a check on it before washing with other items. Dip a small, hidden area in warm water, then place this damp area between two white cloths and iron until the fabric is dry. If there is any colour on the white cloths the fabric is not colourfast and the item should be washed separately.
- Sunlight fades fabrics so avoid placing precious fabrics close to windows.

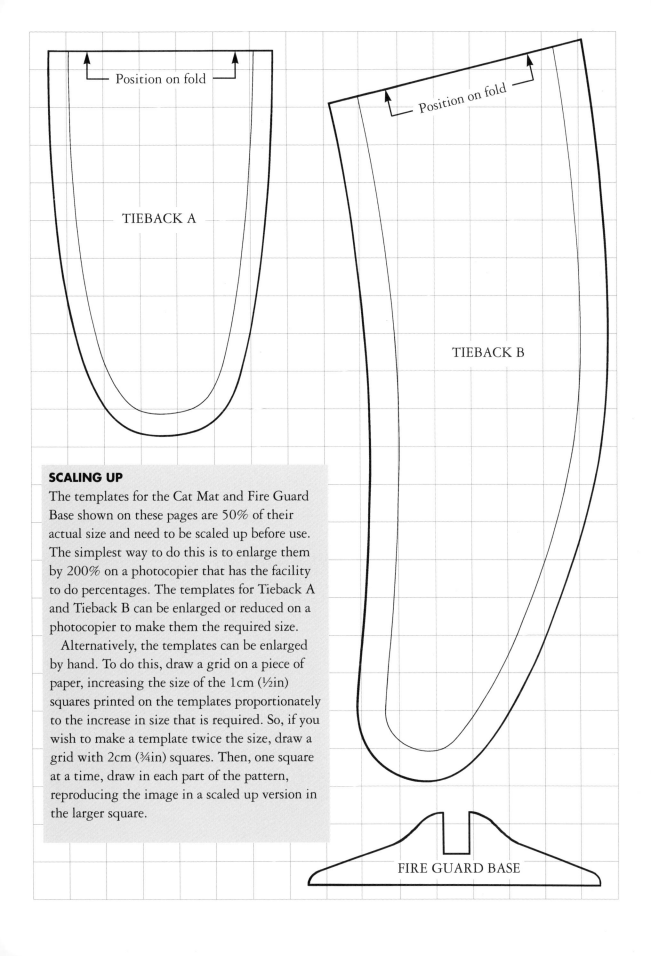

Position on fold

TIEBACK A

Position on fold

TIEBACK B

SCALING UP

The templates for the Cat Mat and Fire Guard Base shown on these pages are 50% of their actual size and need to be scaled up before use. The simplest way to do this is to enlarge them by 200% on a photocopier that has the facility to do percentages. The templates for Tieback A and Tieback B can be enlarged or reduced on a photocopier to make them the required size.

Alternatively, the templates can be enlarged by hand. To do this, draw a grid on a piece of paper, increasing the size of the 1cm (½in) squares printed on the templates proportionately to the increase in size that is required. So, if you wish to make a template twice the size, draw a grid with 2cm (¾in) squares. Then, one square at a time, draw in each part of the pattern, reproducing the image in a scaled up version in the larger square.

FIRE GUARD BASE

Glossary

Appliqué
When one material, usually a cut-out design, is laid over another and applied to it.

Bias
A slantwise angle to the straight weft and warp threads of a fabric. Strips cut on the bias are used for piping and binding as they stretch and can be applied around a curve without puckering.

Bodkin
A large, flat needle with a blunt end and large eye, used for threading ribbon, cord or elastic through narrow channels.

Double hem
When fabric is folded twice so that the raw edge is hidden within the hem.

Flat fell seam
A very tough seam where the raw edge is encased within the seam and both lines of stitching appear on the surface. Ideal for use on furnishings that are laundered regularly.

French seam
A neat, narrow seam which is really two seams, one enclosed within the other. Ideal for use on sheer fabrics.

Grain
The direction in which the fibres run in a length of fabric.

Gusset
A section inserted to improve fit. For instance in a box-shaped cushion the gussets are the four side sections that divide the front from the back of the cushion.

Interfacing
Special material, available in sew-in or iron-on forms, which is attached to the wrong side of the main fabric to provide stiffness, shape and support.

Interlining
An extra layer of fabric, placed between the main fabric and lining, to add insulation, thickness and weight.

Iron-on
The term used to describe the chemical reaction when one fabric (usually interfacing) is fused to another.

Ladder stitch
The professional method used to tack two pieces of a patterned fabric together so that the pattern matches across the seam.

MDF
Medium-density fibreboard is a man-made board which is very strong and will not break up or splinter when cut. It comes in thicknesses from 1.5cm (⅝in) to 3.5cm (1½in).

Mitre
Used on a corner between two right-angled sides, a mitre gives a neat angled join that does away with surplus fabric.

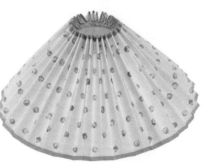

Motif
The dominant element in a fabric design.

Piping
An attractive way to finish the edges of a cushion. Piping is a folded strip of fabric that is inserted into a seam. It can be flat or form a covering for piping cord.

PVC
A vinyl plastic, polyvinyl chloride, which is used to coat a fabric to give it a tough, wipeable finish.

Quilting
The stitches used to decorate and hold two pieces of fabric, with padding between, in position.

Seam allowance
The area between the seamline and the raw edge. The seam allowance needs to be neatened, especially on fabric that frays easily.

Seamline
The line designated for stitching the seam.

Selvage
A plain, narrow strip down either side that stops the fabric from fraying. The selvage should be removed before the fabric is cut out.

Single hem
When fabric is folded once, either to the front or back, so that the raw edge is exposed. A single hem is usually used when the hem will be covered by another piece of fabric.

Slipstitch
An almost invisible stitch used for securing hems or joining two folded edges on the right side of the fabric.

Straight grain
This follows the warp threads, which run down the length of the fabric parallel to the selvages.

Tacking
A temporary stitch to hold fabrics in position and act as a guide for permanent stitching.

Tension
The balance and tightness of the needle and bobbin threads on a sewing machine that combine to create the perfect stitch.

Topstitch
A line of stitching on the right side of the fabric, often used as a decorative highlight.

Warp
Parallel threads running lengthways down woven fabric, interlacing with the weft threads.

Weft
Threads that run from side to side across woven fabric, interlacing with the warp threads.

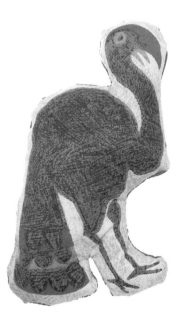

Index

Decorative Details

Credits and acknowledgements.

*The author and publishers would like to thank the following for
their assistance in producing this book:*

Cat table mat designed by Pedro Prá-Lopez and wall hanging designed by Marianne
Garrido-Jones, Treasures of the New Forest.
Stitchwork by Myra Bowden, Ronda Purkess and Beryl Browning. For kind
permission to photograph their home, Martin, Katya and Luke Gorman. For the
generous provision of fabric, Ashley Wilde Designs, London N11: pages 2, 34, 38,
40, 42, 48, 54 & 58; Crowson Fabrics Ltd, Uckfield, East Sussex; pages 2, 42 & 48.

Picture Credits
Crowson Fabrics: pages 6(r), 7(l). Elizabeth Whiting & Associates: pages 6(x2), 7(x2), 10(x3),
16(x3), 17(x3), 32(x2), 68(x3), 69. Anna French: page 11(x3).

Written by: Jenny Plucknett

Managing editor: Felicity Jackson
Project editor: Finny Fox-Davies
Editor: Laura Potts

Designers: Design Section
Art director: Graham Webb

Photography: George Wright
Picture research: Nell Hunter
Illustrator: Geoff Denny Associates

Production controller: Louise McIntyre

Jenny Plucknett has asserted her right to be
identified as the author of this work

First published 1998

© Haynes Publishing 1998

Published by Haynes Publishing
Sparkford, Nr Yeovil, Somerset BA22 7JJ

British Library Cataloguing-in-Publication Data:
A catalogue record of this book is available from
the British Library

ISBN 1 85960 315 7

Printed in France by
Imprimerie Pollina, 85400 Luçon - n 73380 - A